THE RISE
(AND FALL) *of the*
SECULAR CHURCH

Observations of the Church Since
Whatever Happened to Worship?:
A Call to True Worship
Sermon Collections by A. W. Tozer, 1985

THE RISE

(AND FALL) *of the*
SECULAR CHURCH

Ron Fessenden, MD, MPH
2017

EQUIP PRESS
Colorado Springs, Colorado

THE RISE
(AND FALL) *of the*
SECULAR CHURCH

ISBN: 978-1-946453-08-2

ATTENTION CHURCH LEADERS, SMALL GROUP LEADERS, TEACHERS AND CHRISTIAN ORGANIZATIONS: Discounts are available on bulk purchases for educational or gift purposes, or as premiums for increasing subscriptions or renewals. Special edition books or book excerpts can also be created to fit specific needs. For information, please contact TGBTGBooks.com, LLC, 24 Luxury Lane, Colorado Springs, CO 80921; 719-481-1411.

Biblical quotations throughout this book are from the King James Version unless otherwise noted.

NET Bible® copyright ©1996-2006 by Biblical Studies Press, L.L.C. All rights reserved. The names: **THE NET BIBLE®, NEW ENGLISH TRANSLATION COPYRIGHT © 1996 BY BIBLICAL STUDIES PRESS, L.L.C. NET Bible® IS A REGISTERED TRADEMARK THE NET BIBLE® LOGO, SERVICE MARK COPYRIGHT © 1997 BY BIBLICAL STUDIES PRESS, L.L.C. ALL RIGHTS RESERVED**

Scripture quotations marked (NLT) are taken from the Holy Bible, New Living Translation, Copyright © 1996, 2004, 2007 by Tyndale House Foundation. Used by permission of Tyndale House Publishers, Inc., Carol Stream, Illinois 60188. All rights reserved.

Scripture taken from the NEW AMERICAN STANDARD BIBLE®, Copyright © 1960, 1962, 1963, 1968, 1971, 1972, 1973, 1975, 1977, 1995 by The Lockman Foundation. Used by permission.

New International Version (NIV)
THE HOLY BIBLE, NEW INTERNATIONAL VERSION®, NIV®
Copyright © 1973, 1978, 1984, 2011 by Biblica, Inc.®
Used by Permission of Biblica, Inc.® All rights reserved worldwide.
These Scriptures are not shareware and may not be duplicated.
These Scriptures are not public domain.
The "NIV" and "New International Version" are trademarks registered in the United States Patent and Trademark Office by Biblica, Inc.®

www.tgbtgbooks.com

Contents

Acknowledgments

No work, literary or otherwise, is completed without the input of others, recognized or not. It has been my privilege to know many theologians and church leaders, several of whom have contributed to the inspiration and writing of this book. Not all have agreed with all of the text, yet their criticisms have been confined to politely allowing that "variances" of thought and expression do exist.

In particular, I offer my thanks to the following:

Clarence ("Bud") Bence, longtime friend, college classmate, scholar, theologian, professor, Dean, and Vice President of various institutions of higher learning. His critique of the chapter on leadership and textual additions regarding seminary training are most appreciated.

Paul Ferrin, music leader, Minister of Music, national music director for a large denomination, accomplished pianist and inspirational leader, along with wife Marjorie, of "Hymn Sings" across the country over the past several years. Paul's input and comments relating to the chapter 6, Sing a New Song unto the Lord, helped frame the discussion and provided context for the discussion of the praise and worship revolution that is ongoing.

My wife, Joyce, who seemingly never tires of editing and re-editing. Her talents and quiet gifts are a personal gift to me from the Lord.

Introduction

Over a half century ago, A. W. Tozer warned about the invasion of secularism into the church. He stated in a sermon in 1962, even then it was "scarcely possible in most places to get anyone to attend a meeting where the only attraction was God." The more things change, the more they stay the same. . . .

I have no particular qualifications to write this book, none except perhaps that my father was an ordained minister, or that I happen to be married to the third cousin of a pastor of a large church in California, or that I have sung in church choirs for the majority of my seventy two years, or that I graduated from seminary at the top of my class—well the last one at least is not true. I never attended seminary. I am not a theologian. I did teach an adult Sunday school class once. I am not a prophet. My ability to predict the future is limited to little more than holding my finger in the wind and asserting the obvious.

I am not naïve enough to believe that anything I write can add or detract from anything the Hybels or Warrens of the contemporary church world have already written. Their success speaks for itself and the path they have followed has become a model, reproduced to a large degree by many others across the country. The fact that characteristics of the secular church exist in their churches does not imply that I believe they are misguided or unscriptural in any way. I am just an observer from the outside looking in, less critical (hopefully) than concerned, privately passionate rather than excessively and overtly activist.

To state the truth it was oxygen depravation that began this book. I was on the treadmill at the local YMCA, completing my fifth mile, when it came to me. Rather than waste any more sleepless nights arguing with nameless music directors and pastors about the subtle, insidious, yet discernable creep of secularism into the worship experience, and deciding to forego the endless futile search for the perfect church, this book is the result.

Parts of this book will anger some of you. Other parts may cause you to applaud. The intent is to cause neither angst nor elation, but rather to raise questions—to cause you to think, and to lead you to search the Scriptures for truth regarding worship and the worship experience. What has happened to the church in the more than fifty years since Tozer declared, "Heresy of method may be as deadly as heresy of message"?

Many (perhaps most) Christians simply accept the form of worship in their churches as it is. Others seek a worship experience that fits their preferences (not necessarily their needs), again without thinking much about what may be right or wrong about worship—after all, if it's church, it is right, isn't it? We seldom question our church leaders, as they are called of God to lead, aren't they? And if we are not accepting of the worship experience in one church, we can always find another one.

Is there a "right" form of worship? Is all worship right? We will explore these questions in this book. Hopefully, there may even be a few answers, but don't count on it, at least in the beginning.

Many of you have gone to the same church for years, even decades, and have witnessed changes that may or may not disturb you. You have persevered in silence. Others have protested, in vain, resolved to bear the explanation that changes are necessary to bring in the unchurched. For the most part, most of you have tolerated change and accepted the installed leadership as inspired. Others have simply left and started on what in many cases could be described as the endless search for the perfect church. Some have even started their own church.

One thing that all of you seem to do is not talk about it—well, perhaps you talk a bit to family or relatives, but only after ascertaining that expression of opinions will not cause divisiveness, at least not too much. . . . It's only church, after all.

My intent in writing is not to tear down. That would be an impossible task anyway. What is, is already well established. My intent is not to criticize. That would be uncharitable. My intent is not even to provide answers, for as I stated above, I am not qualified to write from a position of ecclesiastical qualifications or education. It is not my intent to be personal or judgmental (well, maybe a little). I am not writing about secularism, or the dangers of being a secular Christian, whatever that may be. There is plenty of that kind of pontification out there.

It is my intent, rather, to describe how we got here from there, how our churches are increasingly defined in terms that are seemingly more secular and less biblical, how we seem to be in the midst of a subtle, insidious, yet detectable creep away from something more spiritual toward something more secular, how our corporate worship has changed, how our churches have changed, and what might come of it if we continue on the same path we seem to be on now. In regard to the latter, I do borrow heavily from the writings of other, more qualified, persons who are in a position to observe trends from a national perspective.

Change is inevitable. Changes in the church are not surprising. No one is naïve enough to believe that the church today is or must be the same as the church of the first century.

However, change that has its roots in non-biblical expressions or values is the issue under discussion in this book.

The first church did not stumble out of the gate but rather shot out within the context of a totally non-Christian empire. In less than 300 years, the early Christian church eclipsed the most powerful empire that the world had ever seen. The record speaks for itself. That's the beautiful thing. We know how to do this, or rather we know how it was done. Maybe it's a good thing to begin again, to have a do-over when it comes to church.

I wasn't there, but I have it on good faith that worship in the first church stood in stark contrast to any other worship experience available, (and there were many). Worship was God-directed, filled with sacrament and symbol, life changing, insider-shaping, seeker insensitive, even exclusive, yet multi-ethnic. Compare that to notable hallmarks of what I call the secular church today: relevant, segregated, professionally attractive, culture-centered, performance-based—we'll get to more of that later.

Finally, a bit of explanation is in order regarding the questions found in the last chapter, Test Your Church. These questions are intended to help you identify trends, perhaps in your church. They are not intended to be critical; however, depending on your point of view, it is possible to see how they may be perceived in that way. I am under the opinion that facts are our friends, and that discovery or confirmation of facts is a good thing. Blessings.

1

What Values Characterize
Your Church?

And be not conformed to this world: but be ye transformed by the renewing of your mind, that ye may prove what is that good, and acceptable, and perfect, will of God (Romans 12:2, KJV).

The term "secular church" is an oxymoron at best—a contradiction in terms. Yet it describes rather accurately what one observes in the church today—a blend of elements and practices that once existed as polar opposites now finding compatibility. Rather than being set apart, unconformed to the world, the church is assimilating secular culture, expressions, style, and values. It seems that the church has replaced, or is in the process of replacing, what has been traditional historical and biblically-based sacred values with secular values, somehow believing that the two are interchangeable or equal.

The differences merit thoughtful discussion. Where one stands or falls with respect to these values (sacred versus secular) influences everything: our words, our thoughts, our dress, our worship, our music, our relationships, our commitment, and our Christian service.

The Values List on the following page is simply an attempt to define the issues by suggesting a contrast or comparison. The inclusion or exclusion of any particular value listed is not intended to expose a generational bias, though some might suggest that is the case. The issues are timeless, as evidenced by the fact that similar tensions have existed for centuries in every generation, and no doubt in every church, and undoubtedly will continue to exist for centuries to come. The brief discussion of these values (in no particular order) in this chapter will be continued in more detail throughout the chapters that follow.

To begin, the value of *personal, corporate need* is contrasted with *individual, corporate preference.* In other words, worship may be influenced by a personal or corporate need or it may be motivated by individual or corporate preferences. Ask yourself, do I worship because of a personal *need* or because of my personal *preference*? One could make the argument that personal *need* has little or nothing to do with *preference.* On occasion, my preference may line up with my need, but this is not typical of the human condition. Scripture records: *"We all, like sheep, have gone astray, each of us has turned to our own way"* (Isaiah 53:6, NIV). And again: *"For all have sinned and fall short of the glory of God"* (Romans 3:23, NIV).

The stark reality underscoring my/our *need* for a Savior seems in many churches to contrast sharply with my/our *individual, corporate preferences.* My/our *need* is for forgiveness, salvation, and redemption. My/our *preference* is to be coddled, encouraged, and entertained. The degree to which these contrasting values influence worship determines both the style and content of worship in the church today. Whole denominations have been created, launched, and sustained for hundreds of years over the tension produced from attempts to deal with the *need* versus the attempts to cater to the *preference*.

Values List—Sacred vs. Secular—Helping to Define the Issue[1]

Tradition	vs.	"Need" to contemporize
Liturgy	vs.	Informality
Form	vs.	Casual/non-structured
Sacrament	vs.	Commonality
Symbol/mystery	vs.	Emotion/trite expression/"openness"
Participation	vs.	Entertainment
Personal, corporate need	vs.	Individual, corporate preference
Transformational	vs.	Culturally relevant
Holiness	vs.	Acceptance/tolerance
Missional	vs.	Attractional
Scripturally based	vs.	Originating in (based on) the secular

Consider the values of being *transformational* versus *culturally relevant*. Here, admittedly, the discussion seems to approach meddling, quickly getting to the heart of the mission of the church. One might say, however, that we must be *culturally relevant* in our church. If not, no one will come. If no one comes,

---

[1] I confess that this chart is not entirely original, however, after much searching, I have failed to find an original source for it or anything like it. I apologize to whomever may have created it or contributed to it.

how can they be transformed? Again, the truth of Jesus' words seems to address this issue: *"And I, if I be lifted up from the earth, will draw all men unto me"* (John 12:32, KJV). We are mistaken to believe that *transformation* comes by association or by attendance or through being *culturally relevant*. Transformation comes only by and through Jesus, who, by His Spirit, draws men and women to Himself.

Similarly, being *missional* versus *attractional* may imply that one is more desirable than the other. The temptation herein is to see these contrasting values as opposites. This is not always the case—the opposite of attractional is ugly or unattractive. No one is suggesting that to be the case here. It is possible to be both *missional* and *attractional*. Being *missional* implies an outward focus, an intent to reach outside of the church walls. That intent, when actively operational in any church, is *attractional* to those on the outside, frequently resulting in folks being drawn into fellowship and salvation.

Furthermore, the value of *tradition* versus the *need to contemporize* raises a similar tension, not easily resolved across the full spectrum of church experience. When these values are seen as polar opposites, dictating an either/or response, the tension becomes obvious and frequently divisive. The truth is that both values are compatible within the church, and both must be respected. However, when *tradition* is abandoned entirely because of some perceived *need to contemporize*, the possibility exists that much good is jettisoned for some artificial and perhaps misguided motivation. Similarly, when the *need to contemporize* is avoided simply because "that is not our *tradition*," opportunity to attract and include folks from all backgrounds and persuasions may be minimized or lost.

There are one or two values on the list above for which compromise is difficult, if not impossible. In other words, fence straddling (for me at least, and herein, I accept the fact that my bias is plainly exposed) is not an option. The values of being *scripturally based* versus *originating in or based on the secular* are the first of these. Most would give intellectual assent to the necessity of worship being based on Scripture. Likewise, most would argue that secular influences have no place in true worship. The values are mutually exclusive. Yet the reality is that many secular expressions and influences have made their way into the worship experience today.

The second are the values of *holiness* versus *acceptance/ tolerance*. In later chapters, we will revisit the value of a scriptural basis for nearly everything in the church: education and training of leaders, liturgy, music, assembly, dress, and commitment.

The value—*holiness* (not to be read as the value of holiness, which is something entirely different)—is absolute, also not optional. The apostle Peter's words are clear:

> *As obedient children, not fashioning yourselves according to the former lusts in your ignorance: But as he which hath called you is holy, so be ye holy in all manner of conversation; Because it is written,* **Be ye holy; for I am holy** (1 Peter 1:14–16, KJV, emphasis added).

Note, Peter did not say, "Attempt to be holy" or "Be holy as you are able" or "Make it your goal to be holy in most things as much of the time as you can." He repeated a command from God found in several places in Leviticus (11:44; 19:2; 20:7); a command, by the way, that is impossible to heed solely by human volition.

You may want to question the pairing (or contrasting, as it is) of *holiness* versus *acceptance/tolerance* as being unrelated, and you might have a valid point. However, given the words of Peter, which are directly quoted from God's command to the Israelites, it seems that such a contrast stands, and at the very least, a question is implied. If one is not holy, then what is one, if not accepting and tolerant of things other than holy? We have already stated that adherence to the command requires something more than human will, thus implying a sacred intervention into our lives. Whereas, being tolerant and accepting is purely a human choice; nothing sacred need be present to embrace these values.

The values of *sacrament* versus *commonality* pose a challenging dilemma, one that seems easily resolved by noting that observance of the sacraments (Baptism and Communion to name two of the most commonly observed) is *prima facie* evidence of scriptural mandates reserved for worship. Yet sadly, it seems that even these sacred observances are subject to secular distortion and dilution.

One church that we visited recently offered Communion by intinction. As we went forward to receive the elements, we were subjected to the most obnoxiously loud sounds (I cannot call it music) emanating from the band just feet from our position. The jarring repetitive crash of the drums and the miserably off-key singing from the "praise band" made for something less than a holy, solemn, sacred moment of remembering the crucifixion (passion) of our Lord.

Perhaps it was meant to be that way, as a symbol underscoring the horrific suffering and death of Jesus. Perhaps it was simply more "entertainment" by the praise band at an incongruous moment. It does seem that incredibly bad rock music played during the most holy of sacraments is out of place (or is that just my *preference* showing?).

It must be further noted that this was not an insignificant small struggling church that could not afford quality musicians or the purchase of more easily digestible Communion wafers (To my knowledge the membership was somewhat over 750 and the attendance that day near 600.) The pendulum of *sacrament* versus *commonality* had swung precariously toward the latter.

Reflect for a moment on the words recorded in the book of Matthew:

> *And as they were eating, Jesus took bread, and blessed it, and brake it, and gave it to the disciples, and said, Take, eat; this is my body. And he took the cup, and gave thanks, and gave it to them, saying, Drink ye all of it; For this is my blood of the new testament, which is shed for many for the remission of sins. But I say unto you, I will not drink henceforth of this fruit of the vine, until that day when I drink it new with you in my Father's kingdom. And when they had sung an hymn, they went out into the mount of Olives* (Matthew 26:26–30, KJV).

And the words of the apostle Paul in 1 Corinthians:

> *For I have received of the Lord that which also I delivered unto you, That the Lord Jesus the same night in which he was betrayed took bread: And when he had given thanks, he brake it, and said, Take, eat: this is my body, which is broken for you: this do in remembrance of me. After the same manner also he took the cup, when he had supped, saying, This cup is the new testament in my blood: this do ye, as oft as ye drink it, in remembrance of me. For as often as ye eat this bread, and drink this cup, ye do shew the Lord's death till he come* (1 Corinthians 11:23–26, KJV).

The quiet, sacred solemnity of these passages invokes anything but *commonality*. This sacrament, initiated by Christ and celebrated by the church for 2000 years, is a moment of introspective remembrance, of quiet reflection, and of sacred communion with Jesus.

2

In the Beginning

Then they that gladly received his word were baptized: and the same day there were added unto them about three thousand souls. . . . And they, continuing daily with one accord in the temple, and breaking bread from house to house, did eat their meat with gladness and singleness of heart, praising God, and having favour with all the people. And the Lord added to the church daily such as should be saved (Acts 2:41, 46–47, KJV).

Recently, I had the privilege of attending the fiftieth anniversary celebration of the graduation of my college Class of '66. The event was combined with the commencement exercises for the Class of 2016. Fifty years is a long time, so it came as a surprise to me that our class would be something other than a footnote at the event. I was standing on the steps to the Chapel, the venue for commencement, taking pictures of the graduates and of our class as they processed in for the ceremony. The reputation of the Class of '66 had evidently preceded us as was evidenced by the question asked by a father of a graduate of the Class of 2016 to a robed faculty member standing on the steps of the Chapel near my position. Pointing to the Class of '66 waiting to process behind the graduating class, he asked: "Is this the 'radical' class from the 60s?" Of course it may be that he meant to say: "Is this the 'graduate' class from the 60s?" but I think the former was more accurate. One can never be sure.

The generation of the 60s gets blamed for a lot of things, rightly so in most cases. In reality, the marked societal changes (some would call it a radical shift) that originated in the 60s had its roots somewhat earlier in the post-WWII years of the late 40s and 50s. It was the generation of folks born in those immediate post-war years, now approaching adulthood and all grown up, almost, who were responsible for what some of us remember as the radical sixties.

Boundaries were relaxed. Behavioral norms in almost every aspect of life were shifted (I have to admit that I wore a pair of red slacks supported by a wide painted leather belt—which I still have—along with a red paisley shirt and thought it rather cool.) Things that had been revered were questioned, challenged, and even mocked. Tolerance, which prior to that time had been a relative virtue to be exercised with restraint consistent within a strict moral belief system, now became a universal virtue. Sexual morays were overtly abandoned. Much that had been hidden and private was now openly flaunted. "Question Everything" became the bumper sticker of the times.

By the 70s, our radical generation married, or not, started families of their own, attempted to settle down, and in some cases looked for churches to attend, albeit at a smaller proportion than in previous generations. Some churches, many pastored by members of the same maturing generation, were ready.

I remember clearly the events in our little church in Hawaii. The pastor abandoned the large, beautifully hand carved, elevated pulpit for a portable music stand, took off his coat and tie, and came to preach on Sunday in his jeans and Aloha shirt. We exchanged the choir for a four- or five-member singing group (we didn't have a specific name for it then) and started to use a guitar to accompany the singing (still no drums, however). It was dramatic and the church was ready. We even initiated a Sunday morning beach service in Waikiki (no drums there either as they were too much to haul back and forth, but we did use a tambourine and a small hand-held drum). And some came . . . at least enough to make us feel that our reaching out was partially successful.

We thought that we were being *culturally relevant* and it felt good to acknowledge our ability to adapt. But were we being *transformational?* In retrospect, it is impossible to say. The good news is that the church still exists. They have reinstituted a choir. A smaller pulpit has replaced the music stand. And nobody goes to Waikiki anymore, except of course the tourists who don't come to Hawaii for church. The tension between being *culturally relevant* versus *transformational* is still unresolved, and in reality predated even the 60s.

Cultural tensions (secular values) have, of course, influenced the church for much longer than the last half century. Since the beginning, Scripture records multiple tensions that shaped the worship experience for believers and in some instances divided the church. The book of Acts records these almost in passing, recording the facts of church growth without describing methodologies or offering judgments.

Note the events that followed Peter's first recorded public sermon (Acts 2:14–40, KJV) when 3000 souls were added to the church on one day. One has to imagine the challenges that created for the early church and its leaders. How did they record all the new "members"? What kind of follow-up was planned and executed? What instructions were given for continuing and growing in the faith? What building programs were initiated?

While we know a little about the early church, surprising little is known about their worship format or worship experience. All that is recorded is this simple sentence: "*And they, continuing daily with one accord in the temple, and breaking bread from house to house*" (Acts 2:46, KJV). One wonders if the temple had enough room for all who had come to faith. Probably not, yet Peter and the other disciples continued to model appropriate behavior for new believers by "*continuing daily with one accord in the temple*" and by going up "*together into the temple at the hour of prayer*" (Acts 3:1, KJV).

From the beginning, a new form of church experience characterized their assembly and worship: "*breaking bread from house to house.*" No other mention of how to accommodate all these new believers, except that. "*And daily in the temple, and in every house, they ceased not to teach and preach Jesus Christ*" (Acts 5:42, KJV); and again, "*they were all with one accord in Solomon's porch (of the temple)... and believers were the more added to the Lord, multitudes both of men and women*" (Acts 5:12, 14, KJV). "*And the word of God increased; and the number of the disciples multiplied in Jerusalem greatly; and a great company of the priests were obedient to the faith*" (Acts 6:7, KJV).

Change was happening, fueled only by the winds of the Spirit and the faithfulness of the disciples. The synagogue was the only "church." This first recorded "church growth movement" that saw multitudes of both men and women added to the church faced additional challenges. Would they be welcome in the synagogues? If not, where could they meet except in homes? And who would lead them? Would the earliest believer convert in each city or town be qualified to lead? We do know that the apostles, in many places where the Gospel was received, appointed elders.

The account in Acts records the fear and disbelief of the apostles in Jerusalem regarding Saul (later called Paul): *"And when Saul was come to Jerusalem, he assayed to join himself to the disciples: but they were all afraid of him, and believed not that he was a disciple"* (Acts 9:26, KJV). Repeatedly, Paul's early experience seemed constantly confronted by jealous dissenters—Jews who stirred up trouble for him —who forced him to move on to other cities and towns, eventually leading to Rome . . . yet he was faithful in daily or weekly attendance in the synagogue, wherever he happened to be.

Eventually, as the record states, Paul became an accepted and powerful dispenser of the good news about Christ, yet still, he continued, *"as was his custom,"* to reason with the Jews in *"the synagogue . . . from the Scriptures"* (Acts 17:2–3, NIV). There is little doubt that the early church was *transformational*, while at the same time remaining *culturally relevant*.

It seems that the early days of the church were the only time in recorded church history during which secular influences were not invading the church, but rather the reverse was true. The sacred penetrated the secular and the change was rapid and dramatic. What we do know of worship in the early church was recorded as being God-directed, sacrament observing, life changing, participation inviting, non-pandering to cultural or personal preferences, and multi-ethnic, yet exclusive. Compare that to notable hallmarks of what characterizes the church in many places today: relevant, segregated, professionally orchestrated, culture-centered, and performance-based.

3

It's All About Leadership

If thou put the brethren in remembrance of these things, thou shalt be a good minister of Jesus Christ, nourished up in the words of faith and of good doctrine, whereunto thou hast attained. . . . Let no man despise thy youth; but be thou an example of the believers, in word, in conversation, in charity, in spirit, in faith, in purity. . . . Give attendance to reading, to exhortation, to doctrine. . . . Meditate upon these things; give thyself wholly to them; that thy profiting may appear to all. Take heed unto thyself, and unto the doctrine; continue in them: for in doing this thou shalt both save thyself, and them that hear thee (1 Timothy 4:6, 12–13, 15–16, KJV).

Granted, churches are more than their leaders, or at least that is the way it is supposed to be. Yet today, the church is often thought of as so-and-so's church. How many times has a successful, charismatic pastor left his church for another calling or retired from active ministry only to find that the church flounders or splits or fails? The church is not the pastor, yet the possibility exists that we have made it that way in many cases. After all, one pastor interviewed for this book remarked, "It's all about leadership."

What has happened to the training of church leaders, if anything, in the past fifty to sixty years? One way to address this question is to observe the changing role of the pastor during the same timeframe. During the 50s, the pastor was the preacher. You who are old enough to have experienced those days know exactly what was expected of your pastor during that decade. The pastor preached! He proclaimed the good news. He called sinners to repentance. He spoke of forgiveness and atonement. He invited response and prayed with the penitent. He declared salvation.

With the passage of time (there are no specific yard markers as in years or decades that define exactly when this occurred) the role of the clergy began to change, insidiously at first, but no less definitively, to that of pastor/counselor. In addition to proclamation, the pastor's role now included therapy. His office was open for business. He was there to address emotional wants and needs, to listen to cares and concerns. He was there to offer advice, albeit prayerful and biblically based in most cases. This is not to imply that the pastor of the 50s was not concerned with emotional needs. No doubt he was; however, it was rare for any church to need an assistant just to schedule pastoral care (counseling) appointments. Throughout this period, most of what could be described as pastoral care was handled during the regular though unscheduled visits each pastor made to the homes of those who attended his church.

Sometime during the 70s, a new responsibility was added to that of the pastor. As growth occurred in many churches, mainline denominational churches as well as independent churches springing up, the pastor added to his resume the role of CEO or administrator. He had a staff, other than volunteers, to watch over and direct, sometimes including several other pastors, worship leaders, teachers, and supporting cast.

With church growth came what some have referred to as the modern church growth movement. The natural extension of the pastor's role now included oversight of new church planting or church by extension, as well as managing the burgeoning attendance manifest in his own congregation. For some congregations this church growth movement took an evangelistic bent with programs like James Kennedy's Evangelism Explosion or Campus Crusade's "Four Spiritual Laws." Others took a more sociological approach and followed the philosophy and tactics of the church growth movement centered at Fuller Theological Seminary, discussed briefly below.

Concomitant with the pastor's role of leading church growth and extension came the dynamic period of marked changes in worship, requiring the pastor to adapt to new demands in "worship" leadership. No longer was it satisfactory to have a song leader (sometimes just the pastor). Now a worship team took center stage and became the primary focus of what was called worship, as gradually the word "worship" became restricted to the musical component of the service with everything else (confession, offering, prayer, sermon, etc.) being understood as something other than worship. The role of pastor experienced much demand for change during this time, and change it did, in many cases relegating the pastor to the last portion of the service during which time he delivered his sermon or homily.

Finally, the role of pastor encountered (confronted) the period of diversity and pluralism, generally described as occurring after the turn of the century and up until the present. During this period, the pastor was (and is) required to deal with issues of women in ministry, homosexuality, income inequality, and racial tensions. He had a clear choice. Were his sermons to reflect the less traveled road of approaching these issues from a biblical perspective, or would he choose the wide road of tolerance, a more comfortable and relational perspective, as the basis for his preaching?

By tracking the above changes in the role of the pastorate, one gets a glimpse of the concomitant changes in seminary training that occurred more or less during the same time periods. Seminaries of the 50s trained preachers—in biblical studies as well as epistemology, homiletics, hermeneutics, interpretation, and exegesis of the Scriptures. In other words, they taught, or attempted to teach, pastors how to study and to preach. The biblical languages of Greek and Hebrew were important subjects.

Then, as pastors would be counselors, seminaries added courses on counseling, biblical counseling, and Abnormal Psychology. Courses on behavioral and mental health issues abounded. Therapeutic strategies were discussed and practiced, and for most attending seminary, these courses were not optional. One must be prepared for the pastorate, which now seemed to focus as much on therapy as on proclamation.

Later, in order to assist the pastor in his emerging role of administrator or CEO, seminary courses essential to this new role were introduced, including "church administration" and "Robert's Rules of Order." After all, conducting a good business meeting was only a little below the competence needed to preach a good sermon. With growth and expansion came building projects requiring that the pastor sometimes became a construction foreman (clerk of the works). Outside the seminary walls, publications (for example, *Leadership* magazine) and books by Maxwell and Convey and others honed skills in vision casting, conflict resolution, and even promotion for the local church as leadership was explored in-depth.

During the decade of the 70s, all seminarians became familiar with what came to be called the modern church growth movement. They read and studied the works of Donald McGavran, known as the father of the movement. In 1961, McGavran began the "Institute for Church Growth" at Northwest Christian College in Eugene, Oregon. After that organization was moved to Fuller Theological Seminary in Pasadena, California, McGavran became the Founding Dean of Fuller Theological Seminary School of World Mission, granting institutional credibility to his writing and methodologies. Along with the publication of a book entitled *The Bridges of God* in 1955, and the organization and systemization of McGavran's work assisted by a fellow professor at Fuller, C. Peter Wagner, during the 1960s, the "American Church Growth Movement" had its foundations.

A student of both McGavran and Wagner at Fuller in 1972 was Win Arn, who later founded The Institute for American Church Growth. Arn became the center of the American thrust of church growth thinking. In addition, other organizations that were direct spin-offs from the Fuller group sprang up across the country, including the National Church Growth Research Center in Washington, D.C., and the Yokefellow Institute of Richmond, Indiana. Lyle Schaller, one of the more prolific writers on church growth and planning, headed the latter organization.

All seminary students of the 70s and 80s knew the names of McGavran, Wagner, Arn, and Schaller, names that became synonymous with the church growth movement. Many studied their methodologies and adopted their strategies after they graduated and took their places in ministry.

The 1990s were a pivotal time for seminary training of pastors. No longer was it sufficient to train leaders how to preach, or counsel, or manage, or even how to direct and encourage church growth. The "worship wars" were on. Many seminaries turned their focus to the subject of worship. The Institute for Worship Studies, founded in the early 1990s by Robert E Webber, was begun with that in mind.[2] Degree programs were created to prepare church leaders for the "challenging task of worship ministry in a complex and rapidly changing world." Webber believed that church leaders possessed the skills for music and worship leadership, but they lacked the "knowledge of the biblical foundations, historical development, theological reflection and cultural analysis for effective worship ministry in today's world."

Notice carefully his implied criticism of church leaders of the 90s. They "*lacked the knowledge of the biblical foundations for . . . effective worship ministry,*" including the ability to "reflect" from a theological basis and to correctly "analyze" the contemporary culture in order to carry out such ministry. It is not the purpose of this book to either validate or criticize his harsh claim, however, just the fact that he found it necessary to state it is perhaps a significant indictment of seminary training of that period and previously, or at least his perception of it. And while Webber bemoaned the lack of theological foundations for ministers of music, he did little to stem the shift to contemporary worship with its highly energetic music and rather vapid texts.

Webber again reinforced this criticism in one of his stated core values given for teaching seminarians, which was "to offer an ongoing critical appraisal of Christian worship," to which was quickly appended, almost apologetically, it seems, "with an open mind and heart to an authentic faith and practice in the twenty-first century." In other words, one can be taught to be critical

---

2   "Worship: the Key to the Churches Renewal," www.iws.edu, 2016.

of Christian worship as long as one has an open mind and an authentic faith and practice.

About the turn of century, a host of new challenges and opportunities surfaced within seminaries. Pastors-in-training were confronted with the need to be "global thinkers," to grapple with diversity issues, and to understand pluralism[3] within a culture that was abandoning traditional values (Some have described this as faddism or trendy.) They were encouraged particularly by accrediting agencies to exercise more tolerance, to be comfortable with change, and to be more relational. Revisit for a moment this prevailing culture within the seminary of the present timeframe with what characterized seminary training of the 1950s and you immediately are confronted with a stark contrast: "Seminaries of the 50s trained preachers—Biblical studies as well as epistemology, homiletics, hermeneutics, interpretation and exegesis of the scripture. In other words, they taught, or attempted to teach, pastors how to study and to preach. The Biblical languages of Greek and Hebrew were important subjects." What a difference fifty years makes.

During the latter part of the 1990s and into the twenty first century, seminary education seemingly came to an abrupt fork in the road, reflected by markedly diverging strategies in the training of pastors. One path continued a strictly academic focus, training scholars, most of whom were equipped to become teachers rather than preachers. The other emphasized a more practical training for ministry, even to the extent of eliminating biblical language (Greek and Hebrew) studies, and concentrating on hands-on

---

[3] Pluralism refers to different ways of knowing things, different epistemological methodologies for attaining a full description of a particular field. Specifically, pluralism in religion is the acceptance of all religious paths as equally valid, thus promoting coexistence.

courses that served to equip pastors in their role of shepherding. The former path was littered with academicians who in some settings abandoned inspiration for reason. The latter path was filled with role models and faculty who taught by example and thus shaped the lives of their students. Practicums and residency programs became an increasing emphasis (following the pattern of programs preparing medical personnel and teachers). Some seminaries required that students be actively employed in ministry settings in order that they could integrate their studies with ministry practices.

Other differences have marked the training of seminarians; however, these predate the fork in the road alluded to above. I recently spoke with a hospital Chaplain about his observations on the subject. He was seminary trained some years ago, choosing to attend a "liberal" seminary primarily to be able to experience first hand the "other side"—his own faith never in question. His reflections were insightful and I think represent an experience shared by many seminarians. Only two out of the five primary professors who mentored him believed in all the five basic tenants of the faith, those being: the Inspiration of Scripture, the Person of Jesus Christ (sometimes the Virgin Birth is listed instead), the Doctrine of the Trinity, Salvation through Grace, and the Second Coming of Christ. The others believed in only one or two or none. It is not difficult to imagine the various paths church leadership as well as worship experience might take given the disparate beliefs held by professors and seminary students alike.

There is one stark indicator regarding seminary training that underscores the changing role of the clergy over the past half century. For many, seminary training does not lead to pastoral ministry. According to the Association of Theological Schools, only "41 percent of master's of divinity graduates expect to pursue full-time church ministry, down from 52 percent in 2001 and from 90-something percent a few decades ago."[4] At Wesley Theological Seminary, the numbers are a bit more inclined toward ministry, as "65 percent of graduates go on to full-time church ministry compared with 85 percent 20 years ago."[5] These numbers are consistent across many mainline denominational seminaries, such as Candler, a United Methodist divinity school where only about half the graduates say they will become church pastors. The reason is perhaps partly explained by the fact that "seminary education, with its focus on personal spiritual growth, theology and social justice, introduces students to the idea that one's calling need not be answered in church every Sunday."[6]

The fact that seminary training has changed dramatically over the past half century does not in itself provide evidence of encroaching secularism. What is evident, however, is the fact that seminary training, in many cases, has evolved since the 1950s to include extra-biblical concentration on such things as globalism and pluralism, in other words, a focus on the role of the clergy in dealing with secular issues within contemporary society. Even the emphasis on contemporary worship styles and expressions in some seminary courses challenges pastors-in-training to evaluate and understand secular influences in worship, whether or not such influences are identified as such. To the extent that seminary graduates incorporate these elements of their education into their ministry and leadership practices certainly does impact the church, for good or otherwise.

---

[4] Michelle Boorstein, "Seminary Graduates Not Always Ministering from the Pulpit," *The Washington Post*, May 17, 2013.

[5] *Ibid.*

[6] Neela Banerjeemarch, "Students Flock to Seminaries, but Fewer See Pulpit in Future," *New York Times*, March 17, 2006.

4

Are You Giving Up on Meeting Together?

And let us consider how we may spur one another on toward love and good deeds, not giving up meeting together, as some are in the habit of doing, but encouraging one another—and all the more as you see the Day approaching (Hebrews 10:24–25, NIV).

You've heard the excuses attempting to give some rationality to why folks choose to stay home on Sunday morning. Maybe you have voiced some of them yourself. "I can worship God anywhere . . . I don't need to go to church." "I feel closer to God when I am hiking in the mountains than when in church." "All they do is appeal for money." And of course the timeless excuse: "There are too many hypocrites in church." (To which my wife's grandfather and long-time pastor would typically respond, "I would rather worship God with a few hypocrites now than be in hell with all of them later.")

The polls are deceiving. Gallup and others who have researched the subject have continually reported the same percentage of churchgoers—about 40 percent of the population—on average every weekend in America. However, the truth revealed in some studies within the past 15 years indicates that the actual rate of church attendance is less than half of that. David Olson, director of the American Church Research Project and director of church planting for the Evangelical Covenant Church, reported that in 2004, only 17.7 percent of the population on any given weekend was in church.[7] Olson revealed overall church attendance is virtually unchanged from 15 years ago, even though the U.S. population has grown by 52 million people, mostly unchurched. His data is based on actual recorded attendance in over 300,000 churches.

Another study[8] published in 2005 by sociologists C. Kirk Hadaway and Penny Long Marier agrees with that percentage, finding that 52 million people, rather than the 132 million reported by the pollsters, is closer to the actual number of churchgoers each week. Church attendance is simply not keeping up with population growth. Nationally, only 6 percent of the more than 1,159 churches surveyed in 2002 were growing at a faster pace than the community's population growth rate.

There are several reasons that attempt to explain this lagging church attendance data. Will Mancini, in an article published in *Charisma News*, lists three such reasons that speak to changing commitment and lessening of so-called spiritual priorities:[9]

---

[7] Kelly Shattuck, "7 Startling Facts: An Up Close Look at Church Attendance in America," Churchleaders.com, 2016.

[8] *Ibid.*

[9] Will Mancini, "The Most Disturbing Church Trend of Them All," *Charisma News*, January 12, 2015.

dwindling church attendance, "nevertheless, people are seeking God."[13]

As churches struggle to meet the challenges of declining attendance and/or membership, the temptation for church leaders is to try new strategies to increase attendance and participation. Here the potentially conflicting values of being *attractional* versus *missional* or *culturally relevant* versus *transformational* may take center stage. Many contemporary churches have exchanged an exclusive spiritual focus for what can only be described as a secular strategy of inclusion.

It must be noted that attendance is not necessarily an indication of spirituality in any church. Nor is lagging attendance a mark of secularism. Secular influences, however, do have a significant impact on church attendance. That is the point of this chapter. The challenge for the church is not to find strategies that compete with these influences, nor to adapt to them, but rather to remain true to the mission of the church.

---

[13] *Ibid.*

5

Commitment — It's More Than Showing Up

I beseech you therefore, brethren, by the mercies of God, that ye present your bodies a living sacrifice, holy, acceptable unto God, which is your reasonable service. . . . For as we have many members in one body, and all members have not the same office. . . . Having then gifts differing according to the grace that is given to us (Romans 12:1, 4, 6, KJV).

Commitment means something different today than it did fifty or sixty years ago. Then it seemed more absolute. Today it takes on a relative meaning, as if "relative commitment" was anything other than an oxymoron. Then a handshake was as good as your word. Today, a legal contract executed and notarized is necessary, and even then may not mean what it says. Then, as in marriage, for example, commitment was unconditional. Today, in marriage, commitment seems to be conditional. Then, commitment meant attending church twice on Sunday and at least once during the week. Today, commitment is secondary to convenience and overshadowed by busyness. Then, membership in a local church was almost a given. Today, membership is deemed secondary.

Commitment is a societal issue subject to the changing winds of contextual interpretation. Not surprising then is the fact that commitment, or the lack of it, is evidenced in several ways. Some of these evidences have more secular origins than others. Some may provide us with indications of a secular creep into the church.

Identification as a Christian. The first and most basic evidence of commitment is simply identification as a Christian. In 2007, there were 227 million adults in the United States. Approximately 78 percent—or roughly 178 million—identified themselves as Christians. Between 2007 and 2014, the overall size of the U.S. adult population grew by about 18 million people, to nearly 245 million. But the share of adults who identify as Christians fell to just under 71 percent, or approximately 173 million Americans, a net decline of about 5 million.[14]

The Gallup daily tracking poll indicates that America remains a predominantly Christian nation, with three-quarters of all adults identifying with a Christian faith, and with over 90 percent who indicate that they are a member of any religion, Christian or otherwise. A contrasting religious trend in the U.S., however, has been the increasing number of Americans who say they do not have a formal religious identification. This expansion has been accompanied by the shrinkage in the number of people who identify as Christian. More than 95 percent of Americans

---

[14] "America's Changing Religious Landscape—*Christians Decline Sharply as Share of Population; Unaffiliated and Other Faiths Continue to Grow,*" Pew Research Center —Religion and Public Life, May 12, 2015.

identified as Christian in the 1950s, and 80 percent did so as recently as eight years ago (2008). While the 5 percent of the population who identify with a non-Christian faith is higher than it was decades ago, it has not shown significant change over the past eight years.[15]

As a percentage of the world population, identification as a Christian seems to be stuck near 33 percent. Christians made up 34.5 percent of the global population in 1900, 33.3 percent in 1970, 32.4 percent in 2000, and 33.4 percent today. As for projections for the future, the percentages remain close to the past and present with projections for 2025 at 33.7 percent and 2050 at 36 percent.[16]

Church Attendance. Church attendance, or more accurately the decline of attendance, has been detailed in the previous chapter. "Changing family commitments" are offered as one of the reasons for this decline. Changing commitments should not always be equated with the "lessening of so-called spiritual priorities" but when they are, does this not give indication of secular incursion?

Membership. Membership in a church—the inclusion of one's name on the church rolls—would be viewed by almost everyone as an evidence of commitment. Yet, it is of significant note that the Bible does not speak of church membership, at least as we understand it today. It does speak of being "members," however, in several places:

---

[15] Frank Newport, "Percentage of Christians in U.S. Drifting Down, but Still High," results from Gallup daily tracking, *Religion*, December 24, 2015.

[16] George Weigel, "World Christianity by the Numbers," *First Things*, February 25, 2015.

This mystery is that through the gospel the Gentiles are heirs together with Israel, **members** *together of one body, and sharers together in the promise in Christ Jesus* (Ephesians 3:6, NIV, emphasis added).

For as the body is one and has many **members***, but all the members of that one body, being many, are one body, so also is Christ* (1 Corinthians 12:12, NKJV, emphasis added).

So we, being many, are one body in Christ, and individually **members** *of one another* (Romans 12:5, NKJV, emphasis added).

These references and others that could be cited directly relate to our being members of one body, a reference to the church, the body of Christ. But what does that have to do with actually being included in the membership roll of a particular church? Is this like being members of some club (Costco or Sam's Club or American Express, in which "Membership has its privileges!")?

Note Paul's words again. In none of the scriptural references above does he state that *membership is like **being in a club*** that offers benefits to its members, but rather that *as members **we are the club***! We are the body! The meaning of the word "member" is not to be construed as a common social or cultural invention (construction), but rather as a medical term as in "members" or parts of the body. Does membership in a particular church really matter given the fact then that as born again citizens of the Kingdom, we are already "in"?

For some it matters a lot.[17] Ed Stezer, writing in *Outreach Magazine*, seems to equate membership in a specific church with being "members in the body" when he states: "Membership is not simply an opportunity to say, I'm a part of a club, but rather a scriptural expression of covenant connectedness to a church."[18] Does "covenant connectedness" imply the necessity of having your name being included on some church membership roll? What "scriptural expression" is being cited in Stezer's statement?

His reasoning includes additional comments[19] such as:

> "To reject the value of membership is to deny what God has already established in fact."
>
> "There is no such thing in the New Testament as a church without some recognition of belonging— of membership in community."
>
> "People need membership commitment because they need to be connected to a Christian community."

Stezer, it seems, has no difficulty conflating membership as evidenced by inclusion on some church rolls (a non-biblical or at best an extra-biblical reality) with being members of the body (a biblical construct understood by believers).

---

[17]   Ricky Jones, writing in The Gospel Coalition's "Is Church Membership Really Required?" March 27, 2014. Ricky Jones is lead pastor of RiverOaks Presbyterian Church in Tulsa, Oklahoma.

[18]   Ed Stetzer, "Membership Matters: 3 Reasons for Church Membership— Why does church membership matter? Why is church attendance not enough?" *Outreach Magazine*, June 23, 2015.

[19]   *Ibid.* All quotations are taken from the article cited in the previous footnote.

Jamon Sorrells, on the other hand, offers this:

> The Bible speaks of nothing of church "membership" as we know it, other than the membership of the *one* church of Jesus Christ. The scriptures never divide the local assembly into two groups, the "members" and the "non-members," or make any other distinction between believers for that matter. Why then, is so much emphasis put on local church membership in our day?[20]

Could it be that Sorrells is right, that "membership" really "does have its privileges"? Many of you have perhaps experienced this first hand as you have noted that only members in some churches are allowed to participate in Communion, receive special aid or assistance, or even sing in the choir. Some churches extend other benefits to members such as not charging for "certain services of the church," while charging "retail value" to "non-members," for the same services (that is, marriages, counseling, education, etc.). "Is this Biblical?" Sorrells asks.[21]

Is church membership a sacred privilege or a secular accommodation? The answer seems to be both, depending on whom you read.

Tithing. Another evidence of possible secular incursion into commitment to the church is found in the practice of tithing. It

---

[20] Jamon S. R. Sorrells, "A Look at the Modern Practice of Church Membership." Dwight Gingrich Online, Essays (Online Articles), dwightgingrich.com.

[21] *Ibid.*

may surprise many that the word *tithing* as understood by most Christians today—giving ten percent of your gross income to the church—has nothing to do with what is referred to as tithing in the Scriptures.[22]

The Jewish historian, Alfred Edersheim, goes into great detail to explain the "religious contributions of every Jewish layman at the time of the second Temple," which were as follows:

> Biccurim and Terumoth, say two percent; from the "first of the fleece," at least five shekels' weight; from the "first of the dough," say four percent; "corners of the fields" for the poor, say two percent; the first, or Levitical tithe, ten percent; the second, or festival tithe, to be used at the feasts in Jerusalem, and in the third and sixth years to be the "poor's tithe," ten percent; the firstlings of all animals, either in kind or money-value; five shekels for every first-born son, provided he were the first child of his mother, and free of blemish; and the half-shekel of the Temple-tribute.[23]

Edersheim makes it very clear that the Mosaic Laws did not apply to all income, but only to a percentage of the produce from crops and the firstborn of all livestock. The actual amount of the tithe would have been around 25 percent of the overall revenue derived from agricultural endeavors. No gifts or tithes were required from trade or merchandise, or from carpenters or the poor. The food

---

[22] Alfred Edersheim, "The Temple: Its Ministry and Services," Philologos Religious Online Books, Philologos.org., Chapter 19, "The Nazarite's Vow, The Offering of Firstfruits in the Temple."

[23] *Ibid.*

being tithed was given to the Levites, Priests, and needy people who did not own land and therefore had no direct way to raise food for themselves.

So where exactly did the notion of tithing come from? When did the church begin to understand tithing as "giving ten percent of your gross income"? It is, perhaps, understandable that a tradition of tithing could have been inferred from the Old Testament record though such cannot be directly arguable from Scripture. Abram offered a tithe from the spoils of war to Melchizedek, king of Salem and priest of the most high God (Genesis 14:18–20). In Numbers, the tithe is equated with the "heave offering," a portion of grain and wine to be given to the children of Levi for their service in the tabernacle (Numbers 18:21–24). The whole nation of Judah was cursed for robbing God of the tithes and offerings (Malachi 3:8–10). In the New Testament, Jesus, in response to a question from spies sent from the priests and scribes, gave this answer regarding a "tribute" to Caesar: *"Render therefore unto Caesar the things which be Caesar's, and unto God the things which be God's"* (Luke 20:25, KJV). However, nowhere do these Scriptures state that a tithe of *all revenue* is required of everyone.

In fact, it was not until some time around 567 AD via a letter from the bishops assembled at Tours that the tithe was first established in the Christian church. Much later, Christian Roman emperors granted the right to churches of retaining a portion of the produce from certain lands. It was not until the end of the eighth century that enforcement of the tithe by *civil law* was observed. In English law, the first mention of tithes is found in the Statute of Westminster of 1285.[24]

---

[24] From "Moral Aspect of Divine Law," *The Catholic Encyclopedia*, Vol. 9 (New York: Robert Appleton Company, 1910).

Today, the mandate underlying the principle of tithing is derived primarily from Malachi 3:10, in which God says:

> *"Bring the whole tithe into the storehouse, that there*
> *may be food in my house. Test me in this," says the*
> *LORD Almighty, "and see if I will not throw open the*
> *floodgates of heaven and pour out so much blessing*
> *that there will not be room enough to store it."*

However, apart from this biblical injunction, this brief review of tithing throughout church history would seem to indicate that tithing is as much "custom as command"—an "obligation of conscience" as well as a "divine ordinance."[25] It was, in fact, the codification of the tithe into civil (secular) law that seemed to provide status to the tithe, along with the indirect references from Scripture.

Reasonable Service. Most Christians would agree that service within the church is a significant evidence of one's commitment. But just what is "reasonable service"? The New International Version (as well as several other translations) gets to the true interpretation of the term:

> *Therefore, I urge you, brothers and sisters, in view of*
> *God's mercy, to offer your bodies as a living sacrifice,*
> *holy and pleasing to God—this is your true and proper*
> *worship* (Romans 12:1, NIV).

Paul makes it clear that "reasonable service" is a volitional intelligent act of the will—that of offering up our bodies to God.

---

[25] *Ibid.*

Notably absent in this understanding of "reasonable service" are the often self-imposed obligations or expectations of believers. Ask any regular churchgoer to define service within the context of the church and you will get responses that range from tidying up the pew racks after worship, to teaching a Sunday school class, to singing in the choir, to driving the church van to and from the nursing home to church on Sunday mornings.

However, "reasonable service" is quite simply *worship,* or as David Guzik states: "a life of worship according to God's Word."[26] This is the first and foremost priority for the Christian. All other acts of service are secondary. Paul seems to be making a distinction between *being* and *doing.* In other words, our lives are to *be* holy and pleasing to God as we present ourselves to Him in worship as compared or contrasted to *doing* acts of service, no matter how good and proper those acts may be. Some may find this distinction between *being* and *doing* artificial or contrived.

In so saying, it is not to be inferred that serving ("*doing*") in the church is less important, for Paul goes on to say: "*Since we have gifts that differ according to the grace given to us, each of us is to exercise them accordingly*" (Romans 12:6, NASB). Paul is stating that our functioning in the church must be according to the gifts each has been given, not so for "reasonable service"—an obligation to which we all have been called without regard to our giftedness. Yet how often do we find our service based on little other than perceived secular responsibilities.

---

[26] David Guzik, Study Guide for Romans 12. From the Blue Letter Bible online, blueletterbible.org.

6

Sing a New Song
unto the Lord

*Praise ye the LORD. Sing unto the LORD a new song,
and his praise in the congregation of saints* (Psalm
149:1, KJV).

It is not surprising that music in some churches today is
very much the same as music in secular society in general.
Recently I happened to be on the sidewalk outside the wall
that enclosed our church's "Fellowship Hall," also containing
the practice stage for the "worship team" as it was rehearsing
music for Sunday's worship service. Admittedly the words were
indistinct and somewhat muffled by the wall that separated
us, but the sound emanating from within was absolutely and
completely indistinguishable from that coming from any number
of nightclubs in town just a few blocks away on any given weekend
night.

One of the more astounding observations gained during
the researching and writing of this book was the fact that one
"successful" local church actually hands out **earplugs** to those

entering to worship on Sunday morning. I describe that church as successful only by the metric of attendance, as I have no other first hand information about their ministry. Now the fact is, earplugs might be considered compassionate and appropriate, especially if one is attempting to prevent auditory injury secondary to excessive noise exposure on the job or at the shooting range. That is not in itself a bad thing. However, there seems to be another logical solution for the church, one that more effectively deals with the challenge of injurious decibel levels emanating from the stage during worship. I leave that for the reader to suggest.

There are more significant issues, other than decibels, relating to music that demand attention, things like incongruity of lyrics and music, forced and artificial rhythms, un-singable melodies, intended dissonance, and unresolved endings to name a few. In other words, some of the music that masquerades as such in the church today is just plain bad. It is difficult to even call it music. In their defense, one cannot question the sincerity or motivation of those who write and/or perform such music. No doubt most believe that this is their gift to God as an act of worship. However, the act of questioning the quality of such music in the church is just as valid as blind acceptance of everything performed, perhaps more valid when considering the biblical reasons for music in worship.

Just because we feel we have "encountered God profoundly at times of musical worship" we can quite wrongly assume that music "enables us to experience God in fresh and powerful ways," stated Bob Kauflin in an article published in 2008.[27] Kauflin went on to add:

---

[27] Bob Kauflin, "Why Theology Matters to Christian Musicians," November 18, 2008.

If God had wanted us to know him primarily through music, the Bible would be a soundtrack, not a book. Music affects and helps us in many ways, but it doesn't replace truth about God. By itself, music can never help us understand the meaning of God's self-existence, the nature of the Incarnation, or Christ's substitutionary atonement. Simply put, truth outlasts tunes.

Kauflin's point speaks to the heart of worship—it must originate in and flow from a sound theological basis, anchored in truth, not in an emotional experience. Music is not the mediator that takes us to God or reveals God to us (There is only one mediator, Jesus Christ, and He alone is the Way to God.) Simply put, worship must center on the Word of God, revealed in Scripture. Sadly, much of music in the church today misses that point.

Let me start with a few examples of what I am talking about (and there are hundreds from which one could pick).[28] Consider the lyrics to a very popular "praise song" entitled "Ten Thousand Reasons,"[29] sung often at our church. Immediately in the first line of the first verse one is confronted with what I redundantly refer to as trivial banality. Never in the history of the world, since creation's grand work began, has there been anything other than a new day dawning when the sun comes up. When I hear the words of the opening refrain, I feel like I am responding to one of the earlier Geico commercials—"Everybody knows that!"

---

[28] Adam Walker Cleaveland, "Very Bad Praise Music Lyrics," January 6, 2010. Several additional praise lyrics written by Matt Redman and others are included in this short article.

[29] Music and lyrics by Jonas Myrin and Matt Redman.

The triviality continues with an encouragement to sing "Your song" again. Just what, pray tell, is "Your song"? I know of many songs of the King, and this does not sound in any way like one of them. *"Holy, holy, holy, Lord God Almighty"* qualifies, does it not? How about *"All creatures of our God and King, lift up your voice and let us sing, Alléluia!"*

Compare the lyrics of the song in question to those of another morning song:

> When morning guilds the skies, my heart awakening cries, may Jesus Christ be praised.

It's hard to sing or even recite those words without a sense of newly awakened joy. Please note that I am not referring to personal preference here, though some would perhaps level that criticism. I am referring to poetic splendor, to the value of words that capture the deepest longings of the heart, words that convey eternal truths about an eternal God.

And then if it were possible, the popular praise song referenced here gets even worse . . . as the words direct us to *"Sing like never before . . ."* Would someone please explain to me how one can sing like never before after singing this song forty or fifty times? But the final redundancy, it seems, is saved for the last verse that describes *in triplicate* the end of "my time." ("And on that day when my strength is failing, the end draws near and my time has come.") Are there any more self-focused ways that one can say it? Why not add: "It's over. I am finished!" And let's not forget the concluding phrase – "ten thousand years and then forevermore." That phrase at least is not redundant but needlessly repetitive. Who alone but God can differentiate experientially ten thousand years from forevermore anyway? It is just bad poetry or prose.

For those of you who find my comments cynical and perhaps sarcastic, may I remind you again that I do not doubt the sincerity of those who either perform or sing this song. Many thousands are "blessed" and encouraged by it. Many have commented on Redman's website to that end. Many believe that they are drawn to praise and worship via this song and others like it, but are they experiencing worship "in spirit and in truth" or just captured by the emotionalism of the experience? I reference this song, not to pass judgment on those who sing it, but rather to illustrate the absence of poetic genius and the unnecessary repetitive redundancy of the lyrics, which stand in stark contrast to other great songs of the faith. For me, the words are like adding to the words by which much great literature begins: "Once upon a time, a very, very long time ago, even thousands of years ago . . ." That is trivial and redundant!

Admittedly, this praise song is at least singable, and some parts of it are worshipful, even if repetitive. Such is not the case for many other praise songs, especially when examining the lyrical content. Some are even heretical as illustrated by Sandy Simpson in "Testing Music in the Church."[30] Under the categories of "the bad" and "the ugly," Simpson cites several examples of these so-called "praise songs." For many reasons they are not repeated here.

Another contemporary praise song entitled "I See the Lord" written in the mid-1990s by Chris Falson contrasts sharply with "Ten Thousand Reasons." The words are poetically picturesque and dramatic, taken directly from Scripture: *"I saw also the LORD sitting upon a throne . . . and his train filled the temple. . . . The whole earth is full of his glory"* (Isaiah 6:1, 3, KJV).

---

[30] Sandy Simpson, "Testing Music in the Church," October 2000. Simpson gives examples of Christian music lyrics in four categories: the "good, the not-so-good, the bad, and the ugly."

And though "Holy, Holy, Holy" is repetitive throughout the chorus, it is not so repetitive as to be hypnotic and boring—the melody line ascends beautifully throughout and lifts the singer and hearer to a lofty consideration of God's holiness.

Next consider an old hymn, "I Need Thee Every Hour," written by Annie S. Hawks in 1872.[31] The music was borrowed from another hymn tune written by Robert Lowery in 1872 also. Multiple settings of this hymn have appeared over the years, but none so lovely and worshipful as one by John Ness Beck in 1978.[32] The lyrics to this hymn succeed where many contemporary songs fail given the fact that they are quite personal and introspective, as indeed are many of today's praise songs. Yet the focus seems to remain on the Lord, in spite of the repeated reference to my need for Him . . .

> I need Thee every hour most gracious Lord;
> No tender voice like Thine can peace afford.
>
> *Refrain:*
> I need Thee, O I need Thee;
> Every hour I need Thee!
> O bless me now, my Savior, I come to Thee.
>
> I need Thee every hour, stay Thou nearby;
> Temptations lose their pow'r when Thou art nigh.
>
> I need Thee every hour, in joy or pain;
> Come quickly and abide, or life is vain.

[31] First publication date 1883, Public Domain.

[32] The arrangement by Beck includes only the first verse and the refrain. The words to the entire song are given here.

I need Thee every hour; teach me Thy will;
And Thy rich promises in me fulfill.

I need Thee every hour, most Holy One;
Oh, make me Thine indeed, Thou blessed Son.

Refrain:
I need Thee, O I need Thee;
Every hour I need Thee!
O bless me now my Savior, I come to Thee.

When listened to or sung, the perfect melding of words with music moves one immediately to a place of deep spiritual experience, as should all sacred music.

Much of the old church music may have come from popular tunes, even bar tunes of the era—how many times have we heard that empty argument? Is the point simply that borrowed tunes are to be excluded from the Christian music lexicon? Must the source of the original tune somehow pass some form of background check to be acceptable for the church today? I don't think so. What about the quality of the music? Can it meld with the lyrics so as to enhance or embrace the focus of worship? Good music has a way of persisting, outliving its roots and becoming so indelibly wed with the words as to make the two inseparable in one's mind.

Another example that comes to mind, and there are hundreds that could be mentioned, is the Fanny Crosby hymn "Near the Cross" with music by William H. Doane, written and published in 1869.[33] Simple, timeless words indelibly wedded to the music, sung and recorded today by dozens of choirs, country singers, and contemporary recording artists of all genres:

---

[33] Public Domain.

Jesus, keep me near the cross,
There a precious fountain—
Free to all, a healing stream—
Flows from Calv'ry's mountain.

Refrain:
In the cross, in the cross,
Be my glory ever;
Till my raptured soul shall find
Rest beyond the river.

Near the cross, a trembling soul,
Love and Mercy found me;
There the bright and morning star
Sheds its beams around me.

Near the cross! O Lamb of God,
Bring its scenes before me;
Help me walk from day to day,
With its shadows o'er me.
Near the cross I'll watch and wait
Hoping, trusting ever,
Till I reach the golden strand,
Just beyond the river.

It is important to note that *this is in no way meant to imply* that if your church sings any of the songs above once a month or a hundred times, that fact alone is not indicative of being either more secular or more sacred. My point is simply to illustrate that there is a difference between good music and bad, lyrics that persist for centuries versus those that will be forgotten within a generation or less. Of course, if all the music in your church is of one genre, performed, rather than inviting participation, and uncomfortably loud so as to require earplugs for the listener, one might be tempted to conclude that the secular has prevailed over the sacred; at least that may be true in my opinion.

It is admittedly impossible for me (and perhaps for anyone) to predict how much of today's music will survive a hundred or two hundred years from now. But what we can illustrate with certainty are examples of music that have endured. Here's another from the eighteenth century:

"Come, Thou Fount," by Robert Robinson (1738)[34]

Come, Thou Fount of every blessing,
Tune my heart to sing Thy grace;
Streams of mercy, never ceasing,
Call for songs of loudest praise.
Teach me some melodious sonnet
Sung by flaming tongues above,
Praise the mount! I'm fixed upon it,
Mount of Thy redeeming love.

Here I raise mine Ebenezer;
Hither by Thy help I'm come;
And I hope by Thy good pleasure,
Safely to arrive at home.
Jesus sought me when a stranger,
Wandering from the fold of God;
He, to rescue me from danger,
Interposed His precious blood.

---

[34] Public Domain.

O to grace how great a debtor
Daily I'm constrained to be!
Let Thy goodness like a fetter,
Bind my wand'ring heart to Thee:
Prone to wander, Lord I feel it,
Prone to leave the God I love;
Here's my heart, O take and seal it,
Seal it for Thy courts above.

One can read or sing these lyrics over and over and continue to find truth, wonder, mystery, and promise, even the Gospel in all of its richness.

Many have written persuasively from personal experience regarding what is commonly referred to as contemporary Christian music or CCM. To this point, I have attempted to stay away from such a general label, primarily because the term is poorly and/or too broadly defined. However the point made by Dan Lucarini in his book *Why I Left the Contemporary Christian Music Movement*[35] is one that many observers, including myself, share. It is this: The ultimate move in many of our churches toward "rock music in particular" has been the cause of much divisiveness, and even more disturbingly, has resulted in an emphasis in worship that is more self-centered and less Christ-centered. Are divisiveness and self-centeredness the values that you want associated with the music in your church? It seems that the answer to that question is "yes" in many cases.

Another way of looking at music in the church is to consider a more traditional evaluation of melody, harmony, and rhythm,

---

[35] Dan Lucarini, *Why I Left the Contemporary Christian Church Movement* (Evangelical Press, 2002).

perhaps a more classical or standard way of reviewing music. Immediately one can hear the objections. Who is the arbiter of what is melodious or properly harmonic? What is the line between recurring musical themes, sung or played for emphasis, and endless repetition that invites passivity or mindless addiction? Who determines if rhythm is needlessly punctuated by unrestrained percussion instruments that dominate the melody and literally everything else? Isn't this more about personal preference than anything else? I have to admit that the last question is perhaps the pivotal question here.

Again, as stated in the introduction, I am unqualified to write this book, especially as it relates to training, professional or otherwise, in music or musicianship. I am only an observer, qualified or not by my acquired tastes and limited experience. However, none of that has deprived me of common sense, at least I do not think so. So let me offer a few common sense observations relating to music in worship, and more importantly, provide a biblical perspective on music.

I delight in creating music. I don't compose it, but I enjoy music, almost all types and styles. I do play the piano rather poorly "by ear," which means I have no classical training or any training at all for that matter, but I delight in playing and in making new sounds. When playing hymns or other Christian music, I am making new songs, literally, songs in which I trust the Lord takes great delight. However, I would never be foolish enough to think that my playing reached the biblical standard of playing skillfully (Psalm 33:3, KJV).

The Bible says a lot about music. Consider a few of the many injunctions to sing and make music found in the Bible (emphasis added):

Sing unto him, sing psalms unto him, talk ye of all his wondrous works (1 Chronicles 16:9, KJV).

Sing unto the LORD, *all the earth; shew forth from day to day his salvation* (1 Chronicles 16:23, KJV).

*I will **sing a new song unto thee**, O God: upon a psaltery and an instrument of ten strings will I **sing** praises unto thee* (Psalm 144:9, KJV).

***Sing** unto him **a new song;** play skillfully with a loud noise* (Psalm 33:3, KJV).

*O **sing** unto the LORD **a new song**: sing unto the* LORD, *all the earth* (Psalm 96:1, KJV).

*O **sing** unto the* LORD **a new song;** *for he hath done marvelous things: his right hand, and his holy arm, hath gotten him the victory* (Psalm 98:1, KJV).

Praise ye the LORD. ***Sing** unto the* LORD **a new song**, *and his praise in the congregation of saints* (Psalm 149:1, KJV).

***Sing** unto the* LORD **a new song**, *and his praise from the end of the earth, ye that go down to the sea, and all that is therein; the isles, and the inhabitants thereof.* (Isaiah 42:10, KJV).

*Speaking to yourselves in **psalms and hymns and spiritual songs**, singing **and** making melody in your heart to the Lord* (Ephesians 5:19, KJV).

*Let the word of Christ dwell in you richly in all wisdom; teaching **and** admonishing one another in **psalms and hymns and spiritual songs**, singing with grace in your hearts to the Lord* (Colossians 3:16, KJV).

*I will declare thy name unto my brethren, in the midst of the church will I **sing** praise unto thee* (Hebrews 2:12, KJV).

The Scriptures enjoin us to sing new songs, skillfully and loudly! Again and again, God delights in our music and singing. But there is a caveat. Did you catch it? *"Sing unto the Lord a new song." "Sing praises unto thee." "Sing . . . his praise in the congregation of saints." "Singing with grace in your hearts to the Lord"* I see everything about the Lord and His marvelous works in these admonitions, and nothing about us, no self-centered introspection, no descriptions of our plight, past, present, or future, no emotional plea for understanding. Just "sing unto the LORD."

This implies that music in worship exclusively sung to or for an audience misses the mark, does it not? In other words, performance in worship that excludes participation for whatever reason may need reconsideration, especially when *all* of the music during worship is exclusively a performance. Nowhere in Scripture do I find an admonition to be entertained by a few as an exclusive and preferred part of worship. Furthermore, music that focuses on "me and my cultural perspective" misses the mark of singing to the Lord.

Note that music in worship is both individual as well as corporate. Again, *participation* is the key here, not *performance*. The biblical injunction seems even to give a pass to those who, for whatever reason, cannot sing aloud: "*making melody in your **heart** to the Lord*" and "*singing with grace in your hearts to the Lord.*"

Matthew Henry, in his commentary, calls the admonition to sing to the Lord "a gospel ordinance: it is an ordinance of God, and appointed for his glory." When we do this "with inward affection," it will be will be as "delightful and acceptable to God as music is to us: and it must be with a design to please him, and to promote his glory, that we do this; and then it will be done to the Lord." Somehow, the words "delightful and acceptable" and "sung with "inward affection" stand in stark contrast to words that describe much of the music in today's church.

The apostle Paul gives us other criteria for music in the church. It is to be varied, as in "*psalms and hymns and spiritual songs.*" I suppose that this is the appropriate place to point out that those who insist that only hymns be sung in the church may need to revisit their thinking.

Paul is suggesting that many types of music are fit for worship, especially psalms (of which there are many that have been set to music), hymns (I confess that I am not aware of any hymns sung by Paul in the early church), and spiritual songs. By psalms, Paul means specifically the psalms of David. Hymns perhaps refer to the prophecy of Zacharias in Luke 1 or the words of Simeon in Luke 2 or Mary's song in Luke 1 (though we are specifically told that Mary spoke these words) that may have been set to music and sung in the early church. No doubt there were other expressions of direct praise to God that were used in worship that qualified as hymns. Spiritual songs is a general term used by Paul to denote lyrical pieces restricted to sacred subjects as opposed to drunken songs sung by those filled with wine (Ephesians 5:18). In all, music is to be the joyful expression of songs of praise to God, sung by all, either vocally or as "melody in their hearts."

Compare this with what has come to take preeminence as the singular musical expression in many contemporary churches today: exceedingly loud, boringly repetitious, jarring and unmelodious performances of rock music, albeit Christian rock music. Can someone, anyone, explain to me how that, regardless of how skillfully (or not in many cases) it is performed, in any way qualifies as "songs and hymns and spiritual songs," which we are enjoined to sing in the church? The question, of course, is rhetorical. There can be no denying the fact that music in many of our churches has gotten sadly off track from the biblical standard.

"Modern 'worship' music today is often way too repetitive and, in fact, tends to send a person into a trance-like state. We are called to worship God with our whole mind, body and spirit (1 Cor. 14:14-15)," states Sandy Simpson in an article published in October of 2000. "Trance induction is an occult technique, not a biblical one."[36]

One talented music director and accomplished pianist with over fifty years of experience of directing music at the local church as well as the national level was asked if music that has it roots in rock music of the 50s and 60s has any place in the church today. His answer was immediate and surprisingly brief: "NO!"

Others are even more direct in answering the question: Why is "Christian" music so awful?[37] The writer of the blog that addresses this question gives four simple answers:

1. A worthy message is often mistaken for talent;

2. Church audiences are often either totally uncritical or they haven't the ability to criticize intelligently

---

[36] Sandy Simpson, "Testing Music In The Church," October 2000.

[37] This question is the title to a blog post by Fr. Dwight Longenecker, April 18, 2012.

(some actually like the music that is being dished out);

3.   Market forces which serve to eliminate the junk in any other market are not typically at play in the church (no one criticizes a praise team because their music won't sell; after all they are doing it for other, supposedly sacred reasons); and

4.   The problem with much "Christian" music is that it is secular music with Christian words—the style and substance don't match up as they would in any other legitimate art form.

There are perhaps a few facts that can account for the contemporary Christian music (CCM) phenomenon, offered not in defense of CCM but rather as a way of explanation. Accompanying these facts are numerous indications that CCM has reached its climax and is experiencing a decline, for quite obvious reasons. T. David Gordon described the CCM phenomenon and its imminent decline in an article published in 2014.[38] Admittedly, I have drawn heavily from his assertions, which are summarized herein as follows:[39]

As previously noted in chapter 2, it was the "Sixties generation of anti-adult, anti-establishment, rebellious Woodstockers and

---

[38]   T. David Gordon, "The Imminent Decline of Contemporary Worship Music: Eight Reasons," October 27, 2014. The reader is strongly encouraged to read the entire article, and perhaps take solace in its sound arguments as summarized here.

[39]   Specific phrases or sections quoted verbatim from Gordon are shown in quotation marks; other portions are paraphrased or summarized in my own words.

Jesus freaks"[40] that were the driving force behind contemporary worship and CCM. Once our generation (and I include myself in that group) became preachers, elders, and deacons in charge of everything with regard to the church and its worship form and content, it was only a matter of time before a form of worship music that did not sound anything like our parents' worship music was instituted.

"Thankfully," Gordon states, "that generation is dying off and much of the impetus for contemporary worship music will die with us,"[41] except perhaps for the commercial interests, which will continue to propel CCM sometime into the future. Unfortunately, the current generation of church musicians learned all too well from us.

It is a well-accepted fact that human nature, as well as the culture in general, celebrates that which is new. But what is new will not remain forever. Once something is no longer novel, it is destined to compete with what has existed for generations and continues to exist. The same is true in church music. While CCM is a relatively new phenomenon alongside nearly two thousand years of church history, it may have already reached its zenith. Novelty in worship is not a virtue, primarily because it discards heritage and liturgy. "As with all novelties, once the novelty wears off, what is left often seems somewhat empty."[42]

Contemporary music writers, while "talented and devout" (a generalization that may or may not be accurate), cannot compete with the best-of-the-best of over fifty generations of church music writers. It is significant to note that only one-half

---

[40] *Ibid.*

[41] *Ibid.*

[42] *Ibid.*

of one percent (42 out of over 6,500) of Charles Wesley's hymns made it into the Methodist hymnal; and it's rare to find even ten of Paul Gerhardt's 140 hymns in English hymnals, even though many musicologists regard him as one of Germany's finest hymn writers.[43] Gordon concludes that it would be "hubristic/arrogant to think that any contemporary hymnist (and we would add song writer or CCM composer) is substantially better."[44]

The centrality of "praise teams" in worship that are characteristic of CCM presents significant challenges from both a theological and liturgical basis.[45] Are they participants in worship or performers? Watching them (as without any audio), one is led to conclude that they "*look* like performers; their bodily actions and contrived emotional expressions mimic those of the entertainment industry."[46] As I have noted repeatedly above, it is the biblical injunction that the **congregation** is to sing God's praise.

Gordon concludes that the "Praise Team is not biblical, that it actually obscures or obliterates what the Scriptures command."[47] He admits that many disagree with that conclusion yet finds that many agree with his observation that the praise team is an "ongoing source of difficulty" in the church.

Compare the praise team of the contemporary church with this description of what one might refer to as the original worship team as found in the book of 2 Chronicles:

---

[43] *Ibid.*

[44] *Ibid.*

[45] *Ibid.*

[46] *Ibid.*

[47] *Ibid.*

> *It came even to pass, as the trumpeters and singers were as one, to make one sound to be heard in praising and thanking the LORD; and when they lifted up their voice with the trumpets and cymbals and instruments of musick, and praised the LORD, saying, For he is good; for his mercy endureth for ever: that then the house was filled with a cloud, even the house of the LORD* (2 Chronicles 5:13, KJV).

Later in the book of Nehemiah, note also the fact that the singers were apparently well paid:

> *And he had prepared for him a great chamber, where aforetime they laid the meat offerings, the frankincense, and the vessels, and the tithes of the corn, the new wine, and the oil, which was commanded to be given to the Levites, and the **singers**, and the porters; and the offerings of the priests* (Nehemiah 13:5, KJV, emphasis added).

The point is that the musicians and singers were a highly select group of specialized trained folk, not volunteers, and certainly not an afterthought brought in to entertain the audience or get the audience ready for worship. They were an integral part of the ceremony. Their purpose was singular—to praise and thank the Lord.

Many church leaders of the past twenty years or so seemed to believe that CCM in worship provided a competitive advantage that would draw a new and larger audience. The fortunate reality is that "contemporary worship music no longer marks a church as emerging, hip, edgy, or forward-looking, because many/most churches now do it. . . . Once something is commonplace, it is no longer a draw."[48] One unfortunate fact behind this "competitive advantage" argument is that it is much harder for smaller churches to compete with larger-budgeted churches. One has to ask if that is such a bad thing if a smaller church must continue to use a piano or organ, keyboard, or even a soundtrack to accompany congregational singing?

Gordon's best comments are saved for last:

> What is "intrinsically good" (to employ Luther's expression about music) will always last; what is merely novel will not. Beethoven will outlast 50 Cent, The Black Eyed Peas, and Christina Aguilera. His music (Beethoven's) will be enjoyed three hundred years from now; theirs will be gone inside of fifty years.[49]

As if to underscore the fact that Gordon not be seen as generationally out of touch—a common yet irrational and weak argument from the CCM proponents—he concludes that our worship must be connected to both "earthly and heavenly worship, past and future." Everything about CCM, he asserts, "intentionally cuts us off from the past and the future," both liturgically and theologically. "Liturgically, everything is here-and-now, without much room for angels or seraphs, nor every tribe and tongue, nor martyrs, nor Israel's chosen race, nor David's lineage" (just to pick a few subjects from the timeless Edward Perronet hymn, "All Hail the Power of Jesus' Name"). CCM exists primarily for us now and for those who share our

[48] *Ibid.*

[49] *Ibid.*

particular cultural moment. Theologically, CCM and worship "is an oxymoron."[50] On the other hand, he concludes:

> Biblical worship is what angels and morning stars did before creation; what Abraham, Moses and the Levites, and the many-tongued Jewish diaspora at Pentecost did. It is what the martyrs, now ascended, do, and what all believers since the apostles have done. More importantly, it is what we will do eternally; worship is essentially (not accidentally) eschatological.[51] And nothing could celebrate the eschatological forever less than something that celebrates the contemporary now.[52]

For those who may wish to trace the history of music in the church, there are several books to which you may wish to refer. Two of the better are listed in the notes below.[53] What follows here is a summary of the major milestones, or bell notes if you will, of church music since the beginning of the church (The relatively new contemporary Christian music revolution will be discussed in more detail in chapter 10.).

We know that the disciples sang on the night before the crucifixion: "*When they had sung a hymn, they went out to the Mount of Olives*" (Matthew 26:30, NIV). Though what they

---

[50] *Ibid.*

[51] Eschatology is a part of theology concerned with the final events of history, or the ultimate destiny of humanity. This concept is commonly referred to as the "end of the world" or "end times."

[52] *Ibid.*

[53] Tim Dowley, *Christian Music: A Global History* (Fortress Press, 2011); Andrew Wilson-Dickson, *The Story of Christian Music* (Fortress Press, 1996).

sang is not known, it can be assumed that what they sang was unaccompanied by instruments. We have earlier noted Paul's injunction to the early churches at Colossi and Ephesus to sing, teach, and admonish one another with *"psalms and hymns and spiritual songs"* (Colossians 3:16; Ephesians 5:19, KJV). Most likely this was a break from the worship and music expressions in the temple in Jerusalem or in the local synagogues, but the fact remains, we know little about any musical form used therein.

Historians of the first century make reference to antiphonal singing by the Christians in the early church.[54] As one reads through the Psalms, it becomes apparent that several of them were written specifically for this kind of use in worship.

The use of instruments in the early church seems to have been frowned upon, in spite of the fact that references in the Psalms refer to such: *"I will sing a new song unto thee, O God: upon a psaltery and an instrument of ten strings will I sing praises unto thee"* (Psalm 144:9, KJV). Little else is recorded regarding the use of musical instruments until the seventh century, when Christian organ music was introduced, which is believed to date from the time of the papacy of Pope Vitalian.

Monastic communities were known to have sung psalms as part of their worship experience during the eleventh or twelfth centuries or earlier, later evolving into chants known by many names,[55] which became the heart of church music for several

---

[54] Antiphonal singing, quite likely based on the Psalms, was referenced by Pliny in writing to the emperor Trajan (61–113 AD) and Socrates of Constantinople, who indicated that it was Ignatius of Antioch (107 AD) who introduced this kind of singing using alternating voices or choirs.

[55] Gregorian Chant, Gallican Chant, Roman Chant, chants by Leonin and Perotim (1160-1240), homophonic chants. Gregorian chant https://en.wikipedia.org/wiki/Gregorian_chant

centuries. Though little used during the Baroque period, the chant experienced a revival in the nineteenth century in the Roman Catholic Church and parts of the Anglican Communion.

The mass as celebrated by the Roman Catholic Church, the churches of the Anglican Community, and some Lutheran churches is actually a form of music that includes parts of the liturgy. The mass could be sung *a cappella* or accompanied by one instrument or a full orchestra and typically included five sections:

> *Kyrie* ("Lord have mercy"),
> *Gloria* ("Glory be to God on high"),
> *Credo* ("I believe in one God"), the Nicene Creed,
> *Sanctus* ("Holy, Holy, Holy"), the second part of which beginning with the word "Benedictus" ("Blessed is he") was often sung separately after the consecration,
> *Agnus Dei* ("Lamb of God").

Parts of the mass were sung in Gregorian chant fashion and varied depending on the day or season according to the church calendar. Sections of the mass include the Introit, Gradual, Alleluia or Tract (depending on the time of year), Offertory, and Communion.

The tradition of carols goes back as far as the thirteenth century, but it was not until the late eighteenth and nineteenth centuries that carols began to be sung in the church. Carols were originally communal songs sung during celebrations such as during harvest as well as Christmas. Now carols are almost exclusively Christmas carols or Advent carols and to a lesser extent Easter carols.

The use of hymns in Christian worship dates back to the first reference in the gospel of Matthew—*"When they had **sung** a hymn, they went out to the Mount of Olives"* (Matthew 26:30,

NIV, emphasis added)—and by Paul in his letters to the churches in Colossi and Ephesus about AD 64. Greek and Latin hymns began to appear in the fourth century along with Spanish hymns and then Celtic hymns in the sixth and seventh centuries. It was through the singing of hymns that four-part vocal harmony was introduced as the norm, a tradition that persists today.

During the Protestant Reformation conflicting attitudes toward hymns developed. Some, including the Calvinists, Zwinglians, and other radical reformers, considered "anything that was not directly authorized by the Bible to be a novel and Catholic form of worship, and therefore to be rejected. All hymns that were not direct quotations from the Bible fell into this category. Such hymns were banned, along with any form of instrumental musical accompaniment, and organs were ripped out of churches. Instead of hymns, biblical psalms were chanted, most often without accompaniment."[56]

The other Reformation approach, favored by Martin Luther, produced a burst of hymn writing and congregational singing. Luther and his followers often used their hymns, or chorales, to teach tenets of the faith to worshipers. Other earlier English writers tended to paraphrase biblical text, particularly the Psalms. Later writers took even more freedom, some even including allegory and metaphor in their texts.

Some hymn writers used this media to introduce and spread theology. Charles Wesley's hymns focused on Methodism, expressing one's personal feelings in the relationship with God as well as the simple worship seen in older hymns. Later, other hymn writers such as Fanny Crosby and Ira Sankey expanded the concept

---

[56] Andrew Wilson-Dickson, *The Story of Christian Music* (Oxford: Lion, 1992). Much of the information regarding the history of Christian music in this section is summarized from this reference.

of the hymn to embrace what might be called "testimonial music" in a new style that came to be called gospel songs, sung typically at a faster tempo than hymns and usually including a refrain or chorus.[57] It is interesting to note that during the nineteenth century, the gospel song genre spread rapidly in Protestantism and, to a lesser but still definite extent, in Roman Catholicism, but is unknown in the worship in Eastern Orthodox churches, which rely exclusively on traditional chants, and disallow most instrumental accompaniment/entertainment.[58]

What can an impassioned observation (few are truly neutral in this regard) of music in the church tell us? Perhaps a lot. In some churches, secular influences predominate as music in worship is primarily secular rock music overladen with Christian lyrics delivered via performance by so-called praise bands or worship leaders. In others, a schizophrenic ambivalence combines the secular with the spiritual, apparently attempting to satisfy or pacify those in the congregation with a mix of the traditional with the contemporary. Still others stick to hymns as the sole musical expression of worship. Lacking in the musical expressions of many churches is what can simply be described as acceptable music for worship as indicated in Scripture: "***Sing*** *unto the* LORD ***a new song****, and his praise in the congregation of saints*" (Psalm 149:1, KJV, emphasis added).

In his book *True Worship*, Vaughan Roberts[59] offers four consequences of wrongly viewing music as the medium

---

[57] The distinction is illustrated as follows: "Amazing Grace" is a hymn (no refrain), but "How Great Thou Art" is a gospel song, as stated in *The Story of Christian Music*.

[58] *Ibid*, Andrew Wilson-Dickson.

[59] Vaughn Roberts, *True Worship: What Is the Nature of True Christian Worship?* (Image Media, 2010).

that facilitates our encounter with God in worship, or in some way moves us closer to God. They are summarized as follows:

1. Music evokes an emotional response that for some promotes the belief that God's presence is associated with a particular experience. But what happens when we no longer feel it? Has God left us?

2. Music performance becomes the primary focus of worship, rather than the proclamation of God's Word.

3. Musicians are often vested with an unwarranted status of minister or priest, whose responsibility is to bring us into the presence of God. When thought to be successful in that role, they attain a status that is far too favorable for their own good. When unsuccessful in helping one experience God, they have failed and must be replaced or another church's worship experience sought after.

4. Music preferences in worship are by no means universal; that is, not everyone shares the same tastes in music. When our encounter with God in worship is believed to be facilitated by a certain type of music, demands for what produces that feeling become rigid. This is why so many churches succumb to offering multiple styles of music in their worship services, thereby unwittingly sanctioning division and self-centeredness among the people of God.

It is most important to understand the primary purposes of music in worship as given to us in Scripture: First to honor God by praising Him in song ("***Sing*** *unto the* LORD ***a new song,*** *and his praise in the congregation of saints*" [Psalm 149:1, KJV, emphasis added]), and second to exhort and encourage one another ("*teaching* **and** *admonishing one another in* **psalms and hymns and spiritual songs***, singing with grace in your hearts to the Lord*" [Colossians 3:16, KJV, emphasis added]). Apart from these purposes, Scripture is mostly silent regarding the place for music in worship. Certainly, *music performance* is never described in Scripture to be the primary focus of worship on par with or as sometimes exhibited today, surpassing the proclamation of the Word.

7

The Work of the People

In the year that king Uzziah died I saw also the LORD sitting upon a throne, high and lifted up, and his train filled the temple. Above it stood the seraphims: each one had six wings; with twain he covered his face, and with twain he covered his feet, and with twain he did fly. And one cried unto another, and said, Holy, holy, holy, is the LORD of hosts: the whole earth is full of his glory. And the posts of the door moved at the voice of him that cried, and the house was filled with smoke. Then said I, Woe is me! for I am undone; because I am a man of unclean lips, and I dwell in the midst of a people of unclean lips: for mine eyes have seen the King, the LORD of hosts. Then flew one of the seraphims unto me, having a live coal in his hand, which he had taken with the tongs from off the altar: And he laid it upon my mouth, and said, Lo, this hath touched thy lips; and thine iniquity is taken away, and thy sin purged. Also I heard the voice of the Lord, saying, Whom shall I send, and

who will go for us? Then said I, Here am I; send me
(Isaiah 6:1-8, KJV).

As a youth, I remember going to a Christmas Eve Mass
at the local Catholic Church. I was not Catholic,
nor was I apparently influenced by the frequently
expressed opinion of my elders at that time that Catholics were
not Christians, at least not like we were (My brother and I *were*
convinced that if our kite, given a long enough string, were to
fly over the Catholic Church, it might get struck by lightning,
however.) Of my naïve and uninformed earliest recollections,
it was not the liturgy that made a lasting impression on my
immature brain. Doubtful did I know the real meaning of the
word. What impressed me was the order, the pomp and wonder
of the Mass as compared to the loose, unscripted, sometimes
unpredictable nature of our very low Protestant church services,
which, thanks to my parents, I have attended since my birth.
Even though the Latin Mass has been replaced for the most part
by English equivalents, the Mass remains the same and its impact
is unforgettable. Rachel Held Evans wrote this recently in one of
her blogs: "precisely because the ancient forms of liturgy seem so
unpretentious, so unconcerned with being 'cool,' and we find that
refreshingly authentic" is the reason so many millennials are drawn
to it.

What characterizes those Protestant services with which I
have become too familiar? Perhaps an illustration will serve us best
at this point, and in it one can easily observe the evolving secular
influences on the form and content of contemporary worship
common to many of our churches today. The denomination in
which my father was ordained as a minister continues to define my
memory of "church." My recent reflections regarding two of those
churches, both considered successful in terms of membership,

Sunday attendance, and reputation within and without the denomination, follow.

Services began for both with thirty minutes of non-stop, exceedingly amped-up (I hesitate to call it music) performance (I hesitate to call it even entertainment), void of any meaningful audience participation except for the occasional raised hands and body swaying typically found in a mosh pit (correctly defined as "the ultimate way to show your love for loud, pounding music") at a rock concert, during which time several in attendance left the auditorium and waited until its conclusion to re-enter. Following this, the pastor took the stage, invited the congregants to present their tithes and offerings (accompanied by more of the "performance" previously described), and proceeded to give the sermon, lasting anywhere from forty-five to sixty minutes. A final prayer was pronounced and the service was over.

For you who experience this Sunday after Sunday and call it worship, permit me a few comments that describe the "liturgy" of what you endure mostly graciously. For you, the liturgy contains three elements, if one can call them that: entertainment, collection of gifts (accompanied by more entertainment), and preaching of the Word. Missing noticeably from these services are several important elements of the traditional liturgy. "Oh," you protest, "we are not a liturgical church. We avoid liturgy because it is not popular or contemporary."

My point is just that: the absence of liturgy IS liturgy. Liturgy, simply put, is the "work of the people," which is more commonly called public worship. What "work of the people" is present in the services described above? Some would say praise. Others would include response through giving. Granted. Certainly, the preaching of the Word. But where is thanksgiving, confession, repentance, assurance of pardon, the opportunity for one to offer a humble response to a Holy God, and finally, proper benediction and injunction to go in peace? The "work of the people" in the secularized church is apparently to be entertained first, to be somehow gotten in the mood, prepared by external influences, whipped up emotionally, and for what end?

Contrast that to what is generally viewed as more formal liturgy—a communal response to, and participation in the sacred through activity reflecting praise, thanksgiving, supplication, and repentance. The liturgy, therefore is the basis for establishing a relationship with the Divine, as well as with other participants, in the worship.[60]

Take another look at the Scripture passage from Isaiah quoted at the beginning of this chapter, perhaps the best liturgical description of worship found in the entire Scriptures. First, there is context for worship: *"In the year that king Uzziah died I saw also the* Lord. . . *."*

All worship occurs within some context, which is both personal and corporate and properly begins there. On (pick any date), during the recovery from great flooding in Texas and Louisiana, or the shootings in Dallas and Orlando, or the election of 2016, or following the loss of a loved one, or the promotion to a new position, or more commonly, during the sameness or repetitiveness of everyday life, *I saw the Lord.* Whatever your situation, with full cognizance of the events and circumstances around you, you come to worship, to see the Lord. And how is He seen?

---

[60] Admittedly, I am not directly referring here to the liturgy as celebrated in the High Church still today. I have left out of this discussion several remarkable and worshipful aspects of that liturgy, such as, the Processional and Recessional during which the Word of God is lifted high, the multiple readings from the Law, the Old Testament, Psalms and the Gospels, recitation of one of the Creeds, sharing (passing) the Peace, and of course the weekly celebration of the Eucharist (Holy Communion).

Next note the position of the One to be worshiped: "... sitting upon a throne, high and lifted up, and his train filled the temple." Humbled and awestruck, worship now commences. It seems to me that any other commencement for worship is shallow and self-centered, not God-centered. Worship recognizes our position, our context, and immediately moves from self to *seeing the Lord*. There is no need or reason for entertainment, no need for an appeal to the senses by the use of emotional and loud performances, no time for a staged and artificial transition from life to the awesomeness of God. It happens when we look at Him.

The "Call to Worship," which follows immediately in Isaiah's vision, is profound, pronounced by unearthly creatures who cried out: *"Holy, holy, holy, is the LORD of hosts: the whole earth is full of his glory."* That would get one's attention, would it not? I am not suggesting that the model given in Isaiah is a model to be followed literally—that we must wait for angelic or heavenly creatures to call us to worship. But I am suggesting that the Call to Worship is critical and begs to be present in all liturgy—in all God-centered worship. By it we are transported from the cares and concerns of our context into the realm of the Holy God. Nothing else matters at this moment. Note the tag line: *"the whole earth is full of his glory,"* a reference to the majesty, marvelous scope, and unsurpassed nature of His creative being. We are surrounded by His glory and our response is to be captured by it. Something amazing is about to take place.

"And the posts of the door moved at the voice of him that cried. . . ." I guess that might suggest that if anything is to be "amped-up" or loud, it could be the call to worship, with a voice that shakes the doorposts. *Pay attention people. Something amazing is about to happen and is happening.*

"... and the house was filled with smoke." I've never asked, but perhaps that is why the Priest conducting the Catholic Mass

carries a smoldering incense pot that fills the air with fragrant smoke. The effect is intentional. *Pay attention people. Something amazing is about to happen and is happening.*

An amazing thing does happen and it is not expected or predicted. The focus is immediately returns to Isaiah: *"Then said I, Woe is me! for I am undone; because I am a man of unclean lips, and I dwell in the midst of a people of unclean lips: for mine eyes have seen the King, the LORD of hosts."* When confronted with the holiness of God and His splendor, and only then, Isaiah sees himself in contrast. He is nothing. He is completely and utterly worthless in comparison. He is incapable of uttering any worthy sound or speech. Not only that, Isaiah sees that everyone around him is in the same condition.

I am certain that I have never uttered the phrase, *"Woe is me!"* but I think I can appreciate what state of mind Isaiah must have been in to voice such a thought. Overcome by sin, doubt, indiscretion, improper actions, or petulant words—to name a few—one's immediate response to the experience of confronting the holiness of God is to cry out in repentance. "Woe is me! I am less than nothing in Your presence, O God."

Every Sunday, to their credit, many churches offer a prayer of corporate repentance, asking God to forgive whatever transgressions we may be collectively guilty of (depending a lot of course on the Scripture and sermon topic for the day), followed by a time of personal repentance during which each is encouraged to offer his or her own prayer asking God's forgiveness. Our corporate and private confessions seldom reach to the level of *"Woe is me!"* nor are they followed by utterances similar to Isaiah's—*"for I am undone!"*—but at least they serve to underscore our sinfulness before a Holy God. Note that for Isaiah, confession was both personal and corporate: *"because I am a man of unclean lips, and I dwell in the midst of a people of unclean lips"* and immediately he states again the reason why confession is happening: *"for mine eyes have seen the King, the LORD of hosts."* When we see the King, we are immediately aware of self and our unworthiness.

What follows is critical and essential each time we are led in corporate repentance or directed in personal repentance. It needs continual repetition in our worship. I am not referring to the activity in Isaiah's vision where the seraphim takes a live coal from the altar and cauterizes his lips and mouth. That action literally would dissuade most, if not all, from future participation in worship. . . . I am referring to the declaration of pardon that immediately follows confession. *"Lo, this hath touched thy lips; and thine iniquity is taken away, and thy sin purged."* Fortunately, because of the atoning work of Christ on the cross, we do not need our sins to be purged by hot coals, but we do need repeatedly to hear and humbly accept, "Because of Jesus, your sins have been forgiven." Frequently, this assurance of pardon is accompanied by one of many Scriptures, which assert the same: *"If we confess our sins, he is faithful and just to forgive us our sins, and to cleanse us from all unrighteousness"* (1 John 1:9, KJV). *"As far as the east is from the west, so far hath he removed our transgression from us"* (Psalm 103:12, KJV).

We do not know from Isaiah's vision the exact timing of what happens next. We do know that at some point, either concurrently, or perhaps some time later (the length of the interval is not important), Isaiah *"heard the voice of the Lord."* Perhaps there was enough time for an offering and announcements to be squeezed in there, we don't know. The important thing is to note that it was the *"voice of the Lord."* Within today's context, the *"voice of the Lord"* can easily be understood as the reading of Scripture itself or the Word of God delivered by a pastor or minister or priest in sermonic form.

In any case, Isaiah heard it, and it was followed by a question: "*Whom shall I send, and who will go for us?*" In other words, Isaiah, you have been called into worship, you have seen the Lord of hosts, you have confessed your sins and been forgiven, and you have heard the voice of the Lord. Now, will you respond? And how will you respond?

In all of this, I see a compete lack of emotionalism. Instead there is a direct appeal to one's will, a challenge to action. All of which is followed by a time for Isaiah's response. Would that all worship be so profound, concise, logical, and transformational.

The illustration from Isaiah 6 captures much of what can be called liturgy in worship. However, it is important to note that the Bible is not otherwise silent about a "prescribed form for a public religious service."[61] Scriptures from as far back as Leviticus, all the way through the New Testament to 1 Peter, remind us that God cares about the worship we offer Him, as illustrated by the parallel phrases found in these verses: "*When you sacrifice a thank offering to the* LORD, *sacrifice it in such a way that it will be* **accepted** *on your behalf*" (Leviticus 22:29, NIV) and "*offering spiritual sacrifices* **acceptable to God** *through Jesus Christ*" (1 Peter 2:5, NIV) (emphasis added).

During a recent trip out of state, we attended a church that had been established over a century ago. The order of service as printed in the bulletin can be summarized as follows: songs, responsive reading, more songs, announcements and offering, more songs, and message. The order of service for the contemporary service, which followed the more traditional service we attended, was equally descriptive: call to worship, announcements and offering,

---

[61] This quote is from the *American Heritage Dictionary*, which defines "liturgy" as follows: "1. The rite of the Eucharist. 2. The prescribed form for a public religious service; ritual."

worship songs, and message. Compared to the description of worship in Isaiah 6, much was missing.

There are several New Testament Scriptures that provide us with a glimpse of what worship was like for the early church, but no specific format is given. The book of Acts lists those elements of worship, though not in any particular order or structure:

And they, continuing daily with one accord in the temple, and breaking bread from house to house, did eat their meat with gladness and singleness of heart, Praising God, and having favour with all the people. And the Lord added to the church daily such as should be saved (Acts 2:46–47, KJV).

And with many other words did he testify and exhort, saying, Save yourselves from this untoward generation (Acts 2:40, KJV).

Repent, and be baptized every one of you in the name of Jesus Christ for the remission of sins, and ye shall receive the gift of the Holy Ghost (Acts 2:38, KJV).

And they continued stedfastly in the apostles' doctrine and fellowship, and in breaking of bread, and in prayers (Acts 2:42, KJV).

Then they that gladly received his word were baptized (Acts 2:41, KJV).

These Scriptures provide us with a sense of the liturgy that guided worship in the early church: fellowship, observance of the ordinances of Baptism and Communion, repentance, receiving forgiveness, teaching/preaching of the Word, prayer, and praise. Other Scriptures in the Old Testament, such as the instructions given to Moses in Exodus 25–31, illustrate the specificity with which God ordained the pattern for worship. The phrase "according to the pattern" is used multiple times relating to the construction of the Ark of the Covenant, the tabernacle, the lamp stand, the altar for burnt offerings, the altar for incense, the anointing oil, the vestments for the priests, and the consecration of the priests. "The guiding principle for Old Testament worship was not creative improvisation nor adapting to contemporary culture but imitation of the heavenly prototype," states Robert Arakaki in an article for Preachers Institute.[62] He goes on to state that in regard to the Jews, "right worship was critical for a right relationship with God." Order, sacred visual images, even dress requirements and consecration for the priests, were essential elements for this "right worship."

Compare that with what we find in many contemporary churches—large open auditoriums with theater seats arranged for comfortable viewing of a stage designed best for entertainment, including choreographed lightning, video projections, and drum cages. Pastors and worship leaders dressed in jeans and casual clothes. It is difficult to conceive of anything more in contrast to a "heavenly prototype."

It is more than the setting in contemporary worship that contrasts with the pattern of worship (or liturgy, if you will) found in Scripture. Rare is the contemporary Christian worship service that begins with anything close to the following:

---

[62]   Robert Arakaki, "The Eternal Liturgy Versus Contemporary Worship," Preachers Institute, September 9, 2014. Arakaki attends Saints Constantine and Helen Greek Orthodox Church in Honolulu, Hawaii.

Holy, Holy, Holy, Lord of Hosts, heaven and earth
are full of your glory. Hosanna in the highest.
Blessed is he who comes in the name of the Lord.
Hosanna in the highest.

What about the use of incense? Most Protestants would be
quite curious about incense. Most may not realize that the use of
incense was an integral part of Old Testament worship and may
in fact be one of the key markers of authentic biblical worship in
the Messianic Age.

> *"My name will be great among the nations, from*
> *where the sun rises to where it sets. In every place*
> *incense and pure offerings will be brought to me,*
> *because my name will be great among the nations,"*
> *says the* LORD *Almighty* (Malachi 1:11, NIV).

Arakaki explains: "One of the most vivid memories
many first time visitors have of Orthodox worship is the smell
of incense. Incense is burned at every Orthodox service. In the
Roman Catholic Church incense is used in the high Mass but not
in most services. Most evangelical and Pentecostal churches do
not use incense at all. Thus, whenever an Orthodox priest swings
the censer and the sweet fragrance fills the church one experiences
a direct fulfillment of Malachi's prophecy."[63]

What about priestly vestments? In the contemporary
church, priestly vestments have been reduced to jeans and a
T-shirt in many cases. "The vestments worn by Orthodox
priests are patterned after the Old Testament and the heavenly
prototype. The entire chapter of Exodus 28 contains instruction

---

[63] *Ibid.*

on the making of priestly vestments. In heaven, Christ and the angels wear the priestly vestments (Revelation 1: 13, 15: 6). The vestments are more than pretty decorations, rather they are meant to manifest the dignity and the beauty of holiness that adorns God's house."[64]

But before you discount this chapter entirely as being hopelessly out of touch with the times, may I simply suggest that the biblical injunction asserting "*spiritual sacrifices **acceptable to God** through Jesus Christ*" (1 Peter 2:5, NIV, emphasis added) requires careful consideration. What can be more acceptable than worship based on a biblical pattern? It matters to God how we worship. "Right worship" will imitate the pattern given to us in Scripture.

---

[64] *Ibid.*

8

According to the Pattern

*They serve at a sanctuary that is a copy and shadow of what is in heaven. This is why Moses was warned when he was about to build the tabernacle: "See to it that you make everything **according to the pattern** shown you on the mountain"* (Hebrews 8:5, NIV, emphasis added).

*E*arlier, we alluded to "right worship," implying that some worship is something other than right. Does it matter how we worship? Does it matter what we wear to worship? Does it matter where we worship? Does it matter if the setting for worship is according to God's pattern? What is the biblical pattern for worship? The instructions given to Moses in regard to the building of the tabernacle shed light on these questions and underscore the need to address the pattern associated with "right worship."

The word "pattern" and the phrase "according to the pattern" occur ten times in the Scriptures (KJV), mainly in Exodus, 2 Kings, and 1 Chronicles, all in reference to instructions given to Moses, King Ahaz, and David relating to how the tabernacle, its altar, and other instruments were to be constructed for worship. Notably the word is repeated in Hebrews where the writer states:

> *Who serve unto the example and shadow of heavenly things, as Moses was admonished of God when he was about to make the tabernacle: for, See, saith he, that thou make all things **according to the pattern** shewed to thee in the mount* (Hebrews 8:5, KJV).

These instructions, though specifically related to the construction of the Ark of the Covenant, the tabernacle, the lamp stand, the altar for burnt offerings, the altar for incense, the anointing oil, the vestments for the priests, and the consecration of the priests, were more than just building plans, templates for seamstresses, or instructions for priestly preparation. They were given *to insure proper worship offered to God*, something considered important to the Jew—in other words, they were a *"template for the spiritual identity of the Jewish people,"* states Robert Arakaki.[65] The principle of "according to the pattern" was repeated several times in the design specifications for the tabernacle (Exodus 25:8,40; 26:30; 27:8). To be a faithful Jew meant that one offered to Yahweh the proper worship (sacrifices) in the prescribed manner.

The evangelical church of today has largely abandoned considerations of setting, altars, stands, vestments, and incense, it seems. Why is that? Perhaps it is based on the assumption that Jesus to some degree abolished Old Testament law, especially as it relates to worship. What are the New Testament passages relating to worship? Finding few, the emerging church throughout the centuries has seemed to adopt an "anything goes" approach to worship.

---

[65]   *Ibid*, Arakaki.

Jesus, it should be noted, during His brief sojourn among us, adhered quite intentionally to the Old Testament pattern of worship as is recorded in multiple places throughout the Gospels. He attended synagogue services (Mark 1:21; 3:1; 6:2). He observed the great Jewish festivals at the temple: Feast of Tabernacles (John 7:1–13), and Passover (Matthew 26:18; Mark 14:14; Luke 2:41; and Luke 22:7–11). So just where do the patterns that characterize contemporary worship come from and when did contemporary worship diverge from its historical roots? Prior to the 1500s and the Reformation led by Martin Luther, John Calvin, and others, all Christians worshiped in much the same way, observing what can be referred to as the dual liturgies of the Word and Holy Communion. The Protestant Reformation produced a marked change in doctrinal teaching and practice, which resulted in first and foremost in the institution of the *sermon*—or preaching of the Word—which became the *center of worship*.[66] Priests were replaced by Bible expositors, and the altar was replaced by the pulpit or podium. This marked a decisive break from the historic pattern of Christian worship.

Then in the early 1880s a more emotional and expressive form of worship became popular in American churches, leading the way in the early 1900s to Pentecostalism, a worship experience that emphasized the baptism in the Holy Spirit, speaking in tongues, and other charismatic manifestations. "Where mainstream Protestantism stressed sober singing and the rational reading of the Bible, Pentecostalism stressed ecstatic worship and experiencing the Holy Spirit."[67] Though relegated to the margins of Protestantism, Pentecostals and other "fundamental" denominations were often derided as "holy rollers." But in spite

---

[66] *Ibid.*

[67] *Ibid.*

of that, by the early 1950s, Pentecostalism and its more expressive pattern of worship began to make inroads among mainline Protestants, even gaining footholds among Roman Catholics in the 1960s.

In addition to Pentecostalism, which came to be known as the charismatic renewal, two other "movements" would radically transform American Protestantism in the second half of the twentieth century. The first of these we have referred to earlier as the "worship wars" influenced by pop music and pop culture or the 1960s, resulting in a wide gap between more traditional church services that relied on organs or pianos and had traditional hymns, and the more contemporary church services that used guitars and sang simpler and catchier praise songs.

The other influential movement, also referenced earlier, was the church growth movement. Though less visible to the public eye, it influenced the way many pastors understood and ran the church. The church growth movement introduced secular market analysis and business techniques to the way the church was run. With the introduction of the concept of the seeker friendly church, church worship moved away from edification of the faithful to evangelizing outsiders. Numerical growth was seen as proof of God's blessing. This is exemplified today by several mega churches packed with thousands of enthusiastic worshipers.

However, despite its good intentions, the church growth movement has introduced several serious distortions described by Arakaki:

> Worship of God often became spiritual entertainment. The sermon shifted from an exposition of Scripture to selecting Bible verses to support teachings on how to live a fulfilling life.

In seeking to tailor the Christian message to non-Christians many pastors have dumbed down their message with the result that many of their members know very little of the core doctrines.

Just as troubling is the fact that many churches have become spiritual machines that rely more on organizational techniques, high tech electronics, and social psychology than the grace of the Holy Spirit.[68]

Arakaki follows this with an interesting conjecture—"What Would the Apostle Paul Think?" referring to contemporary Christian worship today—and an answer:

However, if the Apostle Paul were to walk into a into an Orthodox liturgy, he would immediately recognize where he was—in a Christian church. The key give away would be the Eucharist. This is because the Eucharist was central to Christian worship. . . . He made the celebration of the Eucharist a key part of his message to the church in Corinth (I Corinthians 11: 23 ff.).

If Paul were to walk into a traditional Protestant service with the hymn singing, the reading of Scripture and the lengthy sermon he might think he was in a religious service much like the Jewish synagogue. He may not have much trouble accepting it as a kind of Christian worship service, although he might question their understanding of the Eucharist.

---

[68] *Ibid.*

However, if the Apostle Paul were to walk into a mega church with its praise bands and elaborate worship routine, *he would likely think he was at some Greek play and seriously doubt he was at a Christian worship service* (emphasis added).

If the Apostle Paul were to walk into a Pentecostal service he would probably think he had walked into a pagan mystery cult that had no resemblance at all to Christian worship.[69]

In concluding, Arakaki seems to indicate that we have exchanged the uncommon for the common, the secular for the spiritual, the divine for the worldly in our worship experience:

Thus, it is not Orthodox worship that is so strange and different but contemporary worship. Orthodox worship only seems to be strange because it is not of this world. It is part of the worship of the eternal kingdom. We as Orthodox Christians need to appreciate what a precious gift God has given us in the Divine Liturgy. We should become fervent in our prayers and our commitment to following our God and Savior Jesus Christ. We need to recognize that much of the attraction of contemporary worship comes from the fact it has taken the best the world has to offer but in so doing it has abandoned the orthodox, or right worship, God wants from us.[70]

---

[69] *Ibid.*

[70] *Ibid.*

9

The Praise and Worship Revolution

When ministry becomes performance, then the sanctuary becomes a theater, the congregation becomes an audience, worship becomes entertainment, and man's applause and approval become the measure of success. But when ministry is for the glory of god, his presence moves into the sanctuary. Even the unsaved visitor will fall down on his face, worship God, and confess that God is among us. — Quote from Dr. Richard L. Moore, taken from a photo by Amara Blessing Van-Lare on her website

*P*rior to the 1960s, church was pretty much church. Of course there were variations depending on denominational and/or ecclesiastical traditions, but one attending church had little difficulty identifying certain common elements of the traditional liturgy found in them all. During the 1960s, something quite revolutionary (some would say radical) began to transform church worship. As Larry Eskridge[71] puts it, "The Jesus People movement of the 1960s and '70s generated new kinds of music that transformed worship in evangelical churches," and one might add all churches, including the Catholic Church, except for perhaps those of the Anglican tradition.

To be clear, this revolution was not just about music in worship. However, every aspect of worship seemed to be impacted by or connected to this singular change. In an article re-published in *Christianity Today* in November of 2016, Eskridge stated that these changes were "arguably the single biggest alteration in the life of the average evangelical congregation within the last 30 years."[72]

He goes on to state:

> Where organ and piano, formal choirs, and vocal soloists and groups once held sway over a slowly-changing canon of staid hymnody and peppy gospel songs, a flood of guitars and 'praise choruses' suddenly came rushing in during the 1970s. An irresistible, grassroots, pop-culture-driven force met the immovable object of tradition and sentiment, and the ensuing years saw no shortage of conflict and controversy as a result.[73]

The "praise and worship" revolution was on.

---

[71] Larry Eskridge, "The 'Praise and Worship' Revolution," *Christianity Today*, 2008. Larry Eskridge is associate director of the Institute for the Study of American Evangelicals at Wheaton College.

[72] *Ibid.*

[73] *Ibid.*

The contemporary Christian music (CCM) phenomenon, for it can truly be called that, traces its roots to the 1960s. As Eskridge points out, "praise music"— a distinct form of CCM— was technically different than "Jesus Rock," an earlier subset of music that had its origins in the "Jesus People" movement. "Jesus Rock," he states, was "geared towards evangelism, apologetics, and entertainment"[74] while "praise music" was a "mellower brand of music aimed at corporate worship."

For many younger worship attendees, praise bands and rock music are all that they recognize as the norm in worship today. But such was not always the case. Eskridge carefully articulates the emergence of this "irresistible, grassroots, pop-culture-driven force" that has met and in many cases all but eliminated the seemingly "immovable object of tradition and sentiment."

He cites two major influences in this revolution. The first was observed and documented by Hiley Ward, the religion editor of the Detroit Free Press, following a nationwide tour of the communes and houses of the Jesus People in the early 1970s. Ward commented that these young "street Christians" were preoccupied with this "new music." Ward was mystified by "the absence of the old canon of sacred song" among these groups: "Rarely do you hear any of the old-time hymns. They write their own."

The second major influence in this music and worship revolution centered on Calvary Chapel in Costa Mesa, California. Under the leadership of its pastor Chuck Smith and a young hippie pastor named Lonnie Frisbee, "known as a missionary to the youth of Orange County," Calvary Chapel

---

[74] *Ibid.* [Note: All of the quoted words, phrases, and sentences referenced in this chapter are taken from Larry Eskridge's article cited above, unless otherwise noted.]

"was filling up with barefoot, blue-jean-wearing kids, and dozens of hippies and teenage runaways" who inhabited a string of communal homes sponsored by Calvary Chapel with names like the House of Miracles and Mansion Messiah. In addition, many converts were won under the combined ministry of the "hippie preacher" Frisbee, and the warmth and Bible teaching of "Papa Chuck."

It is of special note to observe that the music that characterized the early Calvary Chapel experience was still made up of *traditional gospel songs and hymns*, something that led John Higgins, one of the co-leaders of the youth contingent (and later the founder and leader of the nationwide Shiloh commune), to posit: "Early-vintage Calvary Chapel music was hardly 'something that made you just leave and go into another world.' In fact, he found it 'boring' and admitted that despite his zeal for his newfound faith he would sometimes come late 'just to avoid the music.'"

At the same time, something Eskridge calls "an exciting, spontaneous musical movement" was beginning to emerge in other communal Jesus houses in Costa Mesa, Huntington Beach, and Riverside. Higgins, mentioned above, recalled: "We sang every day . . . people were making up new songs all the time." These "new songs were not chained to the traditional conventions of hymnody"; gospel lyrics were written "to things like Coca Cola commercials" and by June 1968, he estimates, "guitars were making regular appearances in Calvary Chapel's services, along with some of the songs grown in the communes."

It didn't take long for this new brand of church music to insert a distinctively contemporary tone into Calvary Chapel worship. Soon, not only multiple Sunday services but weeknight Bible studies were swarmed by young people packing the then quite crowded 300-seat sanctuary. Within a few months there was a distinctly new worship experience at the burgeoning church. Some attributed it all to the music.[75]

One of the "stable of in-house musicians and song writers" at Calvary Chapel was Karen Lafferty, a Southern Baptist from New Mexico. Eskridge records that "after one particularly inspiring worship session and Bible study" in the fall of 1971, she went home, picked up her guitar, and applied a tune to the words of Matthew 6:33:

> Seek ye first the Kingdom of God,
> And His righteousness;
> And all these things
> Shall be added unto you,
> Allelu, Alleluia.

Within weeks this simple Bible-based song became a favorite at Calvary Chapel and "quickly spread to Jesus People homes, coffeehouses, and 'fellowships' all over Southern California— and then across the country," and by the 1970s to a number of mainstream evangelical congregations, where it is still sung to this day.

Not surprisingly, it was the major impetus of commercialism that propelled the rapid rise of this new genre of church music. In 1971, Pastor Chuck Smith took $2,500 of his own money to produce a "best of Calvary Chapel record album" entitled then as "The Everlastin' Living Jesus Music Concert," later simply known

---

[75] Tommy Coomes, a member of a down-on-its-luck hippie band named Love Song, recalled visiting the church for the first time and finding the music there utterly unique: "It was a music which drew people into the Lord's presence." Quoted by Larry Eskridge in "The Praise and Worship Revolution."

as "Maranatha! 1." Following this, Maranatha! Music Inc., which initially featured Calvary Chapel artists and song collections in multiple albums, was created. Maranatha! Music Inc. rapidly became a significant publishing entity "distributing Calvary Chapel sheet music and songbooks across North America." As Eskridge put it, "A new era of worship" had begun.

The impact of these above events, unknown and unobserved at the time by a majority of evangelical Christians,[76] produced a movement, later to evolve into very public "worship wars" that spread across America. It is hard to conceive of a more dramatic influence on Christian worship, except of course for the events that quietly ushered in the church in the book of Acts, or the changes that came with the Reformation alluded to in previous chapters.

What started as the gentle "Jesus People movement of the 1960s and 70s," with its music styles borrowed almost exclusively from secular roots, resulted in a transformed worship experience for most all evangelical churchgoers. Eskridge concludes: "As the debris has begun to settle and as generations have waxed and waned, it is clear that Protestant musical expression (and worship) has irrevocably changed."

Once content with hymnbooks, now no church is without big-screens and video projectors. Once content with organ- or piano-led hymns and congregational singing, now gyrating "worship teams wielding guitars and electronic keyboards" strive to overpower center stage drummers in Plexiglas cages. And preaching of the Word, once the focal point of worship, has morphed into

---

[76] Ask any Christian today (2017) if they remember Chuck Smith or Calvary Chapel or possibly even Maranatha! Music, and most, living east of the Rocky Mountains, will say they do not, or at best, have only a vague recollection of how and where this all began.

after-thoughts of positive messages of encouragement for daily living. The "work of the people" (liturgy) during worship is often reduced to being entertained in comfortable theater seats bathed with subdued lighting, absent much of the "work" of worship that formerly included being called to worship, individual and corporate confession, pronouncement of the assurance of pardon, presentation of the Word, celebration of the Eucharist, and opportunity to respond. The cross, once centrally placed and visible to all worshipers, is now covered over or replaced with curtains that help to absorb sound from exceedingly loud bands. In many cases, *separate* worship services are now offered to meet the preferences of congregants for traditional, contemporary, or "blended" worship, an uneasy compromise at best.

10

Dressed for Church

You are looking at outward appearances. If anyone is confident that he belongs to Christ, he should reflect on this again: Just as he himself belongs to Christ, so too do we (2 Corinthians 10:7, NET).

Do not judge according to external appearance, but judge with proper judgment (John 7:24, NET).

"We tried to dress like them, look like them, entertain them so that they would come. . . . And in some cases they came." That's how one pastor I spoke with described the transition to a more contemporary worship experience in his church.

The matter of dress, at least in certain venues, is one area in which society in general does not seem to have a challenge with propriety. Folks dress up to attend the symphony. They would never think about showing up at the horse races at Belmont or the Kentucky Derby or Saratoga without appropriate and may I say traditional dress. Graduations, award ceremonies, banquets, even political gatherings, and a whole host of other public assemblies are attended by folks whose dress is appropriate to the venue.

With regard to the church, standards of dress, if there ever were any, seem to have disappeared. When it comes to church, anything will do. "God accepts me just as I am," many say. That may be so, but what has happened to respect for tradition, respect for the institution, and respect for others around you? While it may be true that God accepts me just as I am, and that while others look on outward appearances, God looks on the heart, that in itself is not a permission slip for tackiness or abandoning good judgment.

A Pastor Emeritus in our town was known to have such respect for the Word of God that even during times of personal study and preparation for Sunday morning messages he would put on his suit and tie before entering his office. Today, pastors, song leaders, praise band performers, and almost anyone else found up front or on the stage can be seen in all forms of shabby dress, including "holy" jeans, T-shirts, muscle shirts, even funky combinations (jeans with sport coats, etc.). So much for "priestly vestments."

I learned something of respect some time ago as a newly commissioned lieutenant Flight Surgeon in the Navy. Thirty-five of us arrived at Pensacola Naval Air Station to begin our "basic" training before assignment to stations with the fleet around the world. We were fresh out of the 60s, carefree, cocky, and unimpressed with military discipline. It was about the two-week mark into our stay that we all received a summons to meet the NAS Commanding Officer. I will never forget the chilling effect his opening remarks had on me, and even to this day, I shudder to think he was talking to me personally. "You shaggy-haired pukes. You make me sick . . . " he began. Remember, this was a group of doctors to whom he was speaking. Whatever he said after that, I have long since forgotten. His words, though personal and poignant, attempted to address a problem carelessly expressed by all of us and shame us (Of course, we all silently dared him to throw us out, something we knew he would not do, as he needed the bodies to fill slots.) What he was speaking to, I believe, was respect. We disrespected authority. We disrespected the institution. We disrespected our peers and everyone else who was there voluntarily or otherwise. And we showed it by the way we dressed and groomed ourselves. He was right, absolutely right!

In the church, respect for authority is not something that frequently becomes an issue. However, respect for the institution and respect for peers, or lack of it, are routinely on display, especially in the area of dress. Growing up in the church, we were taught that worship demanded our best, and that included our best looks, our best dress, as well as our best behavior. We wouldn't consider wearing the same thing to church that we wore to the ballgame on Friday night. We would never dare to wear to church what we wore to the beach. A separate pair of shoes (does anyone remember "Sunday shoes"?) was reserved just for Sunday wear. And for sure, we would never consider wearing tattered, worn (no matter how stylish we felt they were) jeans. It just didn't happen. Why? We were taught to respect the institution. Church was set apart. Church was different than any other activity of the week. You dressed up to go to church. And just as importantly, we were taught to respect others, our peers, regardless of age. If it was important to Ms. Jones (every church back then had a Ms. Jones or someone like her), it must have been important to God. Ms. Jones apparently served on God's behalf to insure that everyone looked good on Sunday morning . . . and let us know, not so privately, when we missed the mark.

I am not referring herein to the inability to dress properly secondary to ability or wealth or income. One can get better clothes in our church-sponsored mission that provides clothes to the destitute than what are worn intentionally by many churchgoers. In particular, I am referring to dress as it relates to those who lead in worship or assume positions of leadership "up front." Is it too much to ask to cut your hair once in a while or dress as if you are about to have an audience with the King? . . . I know, God is more concerned with the heart than with outward appearances. But I'm not talking about God here. I am talking about simple respect for the institution and for those around us—our peers. These are transcendent values, values that seem not to have been taught to many of the contemporary generation of church leaders.

One Sunday morning as the choir (over 100 individuals proudly and smartly dressed with full brilliant blue robes and gold stoles) was finishing final preparations for the worship service, we were joined in the rehearsal room by the "praise team" due to lead in the contemporary service that followed our traditional service. I was literally shocked to note the contrast in dress—torn and frayed jeans, with wide holes at the knees and thighs, muscle T-shirts, mismatched coats, and pants or shorts. Were we going to the same church or were some heading off to a rock concert and just happened to stop by for introductions? Not many seemed offended or concerned (I am referring to choir members) and certainly no one said anything, if they thought it. We all have become so polite and mannered these days. . . .

Recently, my wife and I had the opportunity to attend Sunday morning worship at a small church close to where both of us grew up nearly a half century ago. Returning "home" is always nostalgic, recalling memories of how things used to be and reminding us of how old we have become. Worship at this particular church was offered in two services, "Rich Traditional" and "Contemporary Praise." We attended the earlier "Rich

Traditional" service. We arrived early and were delighted to find a few folks with whom we shared some memories.

Arriving early also means that one gets to observe the final preparations being made for the service to follow. One individual seemed particularly busy with arranging a portable music stand in front of the podium, checking the projection system, testing the microphones, and adjusting the sound. It seemed obvious from his dress that his responsibilities may have included janitorial services also—blue jeans, shirt untucked (not specifically designed to be worn that way), and sloppy, well-worn shoes. What a shocked surprise to soon discover that this was the pastor for the morning. Perhaps his dress fit in more appropriately with those attending the "Contemporary Praise" service to follow. We didn't stay to find out. It was notable, however, that the congregation was for the most part "dressed for church": some men with jackets and ties, most men with dress slacks and shirts worn appropriately tucked in, and the ladies with dresses (a few with slacks). We did not find anything approaching "rich" or "traditional" about the pastor's dress. If anything, his dress was disrespectful for the venue and most certainly disrespectful to the other members of the congregation.

Many questions came to mind, distracting me from the sermon, admittedly. Was this his best dress? Was this the best he could do in the presence of the King of kings? Was he really so untaught and undisciplined as to find his appearance acceptable almost anywhere in public, not to mention up front in leadership of a congregation of older (admittedly) believers?

The reality on display with this thirty-one-year-old pastor is not just an indicator of the encroachment of secular values in the church. The reality is that contemporary values with regard to dress reflect not only a lack of respect for the office as well as for one's peers, but also the absence of proper training that begins in the home. One young man, not yet twenty, recently joined our choir. When complimented by my wife on his dress one Sunday morning, his response was immediate: "Thank you, but I wouldn't dress this way unless I had to," the implication being that his parents had done their part, and he had more or less graciously followed their instruction.

11

Where Is It All Going — Where Will It End?

Upon this rock I will build my church; and the gates of hell shall not prevail against it (Matthew 16:18, KJV).

When the preferences of the church members are greater than their passion for the gospel, the church is dying. —Thom Rainer

The church will never fail, of that I am certain. Equally certain am I that certain elements of the contemporary church (the secular church, if you will) will not survive. Here's why. Secularism is dynamic, never static. It is constantly shifting. Secularism is driven by popular demand, by emotional sentiment. What exists today may persist for a decade or less, OR it may last for a hundred years. Who can say? Secular influences in the church, likewise, are not static. They are dynamic, trendy, faddish. Today it's the sloppy dress, tomorrow it may be suits and ties. Today it's the praise band, tomorrow it may be the choir—or did I get that backward?

The point is we cannot be certain regarding secular standards, values, and influences. They are like shifting sand. A church's worship experience and expression, which adopts and models itself on those standards, values, and influences, is likewise just as shifty and temporary. If the model for worship in your church is performance versus participation, acceptance and tolerance versus holiness, inclusive versus exclusive, common and everyday versus uncommonly sacramental, emotional and trite versus symbolic and mysterious, it is no doubt subject to the changing influences of society in general, perhaps even dominated by them.

The fact that your church's worship experience may be characterized by one or more of the secular values described in the preceding chapters does not in itself mean that your church is more secular than spiritual. No judgment is implied, nor should one be inferred. It does mean, however, that secular influences underscore some (or much) of what the church today calls worship. And thereby, certain conclusions can be drawn:

- Worship based on or originating from secular values and influences is shifty and temporary, similar to a foundationless house built on sand. Like a *"foolish man, which built his house upon the sand: And the rain descended, and the floods came, and the winds blew, and beat upon that house; and it fell: and great was the fall of it"* (Matthew 7:26–27, KJV).

- A leader who initiates or perpetuates a worship experience based on or originating from secular values and influences could also be likened to a *"foolish man, which built his house upon the sand"*

(Matthew 7:26, KJV). While that statement may sound exceedingly harsh, the reader is again reminded, "it is all about leadership." Those of us in the congregation or audience have little to say about the format and content of worship (liturgy, if you will) or the choice of music used in worship.

- Worship based on secular values is, without question, divisive.[77] Just as the introduction of rock music into the worship experience has divided and continues to divide churches, so also has the introduction of informality, commonality, and cultural relevance. Divisiveness, regardless of the cause, or for whatever the motivation, can never be a good thing in the church.

- Worship that is scripturally based is incompatible (inconsistent) with worship originating in or based on the secular. Again, values like *participation* versus *performance*, and *need* versus *preference* come to mind.

- Music in the church is "ordained" for *one purpose*: It is "appointed for His glory...with a design to please Him, and to promote His glory," and when "we do this . . . it will be done to the Lord" (Matthew Henry). Music of this caliber (design) will last. It will not be subject to the whims of contemporary expression or faddishness of secular experience.

- Worship traditions are to be celebrated, not shunned. Collective recitation of the Lord's Prayer and one of the great creeds of the faith read or spoken in unison are examples. It may indeed

---

[77] *Ibid*, Lucarini.

be acceptable to introduce more contemporary elements into worship such as "praise bands," electric instruments, and amplified percussion, given the fact that they invite participation and are not used exclusively in performance.[78]

- It is to be accepted that the sacraments and symbols of worship remain mysterious. To reduce them to commonality invites triviality and triteness, emotionalism, and baseness.

Following a worship leader conference earlier last year (2016), an observer noted a "troubling theme" among modern worship trends. "It's the theme of performance-ism," wrote Jamie Brown, where the worship leader is seen as the performer, the congregation becomes the audience, and the sanctuary is the concert hall.[79] He went on to say, "If this current generation of worship leaders doesn't change this theme, then corporate worship in evangelicalism really is headed for a major crash."

---

[78] One Sunday, just prior to worship in the large church my wife and I attend, an announcement was made considering an option of replacing the beautiful raised pulpit in the chancel of the church with a Plexiglas drum cage. The pastor would thereafter be able to preach from a small lectern, thus allowing him more freedom to move about the stage as desired, and the musicians would be able to use unamplified percussion within the confines of the cage—something we were led to believe was an improvement, both for performance by the drummer and listening by the congregation. Input was requested from the members. It is with great joy that I can report that we never heard another word (not a syllable) publically regarding this consideration and that has been some years ago. Sadly however, a small lectern has now replaced the ornate raised pulpit, which is used only for special occasions or for visiting dignitaries.

[79] Jamie Brown, "Is Evangelical Worship Headed for a Huge Crash?" October 21, 2016.

What is the destiny of the secular church? It is impossible for me to say with any degree of certainty. I can suggest, however, that continuing down a path that has its origins in secularism, that models itself after secular experience, and that incorporates secular practices and values is not a viable path for the church to take. At some point, and who can say when that juncture will occur, the path will lead to a point of no return. As the secular becomes so commonplace within the church, it becomes virtually indistinguishable from that which is spiritual. Perhaps we have reached that point already in some cases.

For example, the proliferation and dominance of Christian rock music in the church have become so commonplace and accepted that it has become a genre of its own on music Internet sites. The fact that Christian rock is virtually indistinguishable from secular rock (in every facet other than perhaps some of the lyrics) is proof of that fact. Should this lack of distinction matter? I think it does matter.

It matters in the most basic of ways, beginning with the definition of words. The *Oxford American Dictionary* defines "secular" as "denoting attitudes, activities, or other things that have not religious or spiritual basis." The point has been made again and again that rock music has and always will have secular roots, that is, it does not have a religious or spiritual basis. There is no disputing that fact. Can anyone provide a rational argument for why such an "activity" has any place in the church?[80] This phenomenon is logic defying.

As Christians, we delight in God's explicit promise that the church will prevail against all odds (Matthew 16:18); we rejoice

---

[80] A similar point is captured in the title of the book *Can We Rock the Gospel?* by John Blanchard and Dan Lucarini (Evangelical Press, 2006), a book that sits on my desk, yet intentionally has not been read until this book was finished.

in the fact that He will be with us always (Matthew 28:18–20); and we are confident that He shall reign from His heavenly throne until all His enemies are under His feet (1 Corinthians 15:24–26; Hebrews 10:12–13). Yet it seems that when it comes to worshiping Him, we reject the explicit instructions He has given for how that is to happen and adopt the values and standards patterned after the pagans around us. Though our intentions may be good, we all know the outcome of following those. It is like saying, "I believe in the Bible," but at the same time ignoring the very substance the Bible provides for informing our worship.

In saying this, I am not at all suggesting that we need to restore the Old Testament model of worship, including the prominence of music in leading worship found throughout Exodus, Leviticus, and Numbers (Although the selection, training, and payment of musicians and singers found in those books may be a model that we might want to consider.)[81] The advent of Christ has changed all that:

> *But Christ being come an high priest of good things to come, by a greater and more perfect tabernacle, not made with hands, that is to say, not of this building* (Hebrews 9:11, KJV).

However, abandoning entirely the model of worship given to us in Scripture does not seem like a good idea either. Much can be gained by incorporating the model of Old Testament worship with the high priestly ministry of Christ.

---

[81] *"All the people of the land rejoiced, and sounded with trumpets, also the **singers** with instruments of musick, and such as taught to sing praise"* (2 Chronicles 23:13, KJV, emphasis added) (The word "singers" occurs 38 times in the KJV Bible.)

One large and very successful mid-western church spoken of in a prior chapter recently fired the music and worship leader. One of the members of the Board reported that the Pastor was instructed to "reintroduce" the congregation to hymns and worship songs more appropriate to sacred worship. It seems that Tozer's words over a half century ago were being heard and responded to when he wrote[82] and preached on the topic of worship. His words were both descriptive of the times and prophetic of what was to come as *he stated in 1962* that church members "want to be entertained *while they are edified.*"[83] It does cause one to wonder, if Tozer's criticisms of worship in the evangelical church in the 1950s and 1960s were sharp and cutting, what might they be today? Observe for a moment his reflections:

> What has happened to our worship? . . . Did you know that the often-quoted Jean-Paul Sartre describes his turning to philosophy and hopelessness as a turning away from a ***secularistic*** [emphasis added] church? He says, "I did not recognize in the fashionable God who was taught me, Him who was waiting for my soul. I needed a Creator; I was given a big businessman!"
>
> Let me say two things here. First, ***I do not believe it is necessarily true that we are worshipping God when we are making a lot of***

---

[82] A. W. Tozer, *Whatever Happened to Worship?* including "Worship: the Missing Jewel in the Evangelical Church." Compiled and edited by Gerald B Smith, WingSpread Publishers Edition, 2006, 2012 (First Christian Publications, Inc. Edition, 1985).

[83] Mike Livingstone, "The Heresy of Worshiptainment." mikelivingstone. com.

racket [emphasis added]. But not infrequently worship is audible. . . .

Second, I would warn those who are cultured, quiet, self-possessed, poised and sophisticated, that if they are embarrassed in church when some happy Christian says "Amen!" they may actually be in need of some spiritual enlightenment. The worshipping saints of God in the body of Christ have often been a little bit noisy. . . .

Oh, brother or sister, God calls us to worship, but *in many instances we are in entertainment, just running a poor second to the theaters. That is where we are, even in the evangelical churches, and I don't mind telling you that most of the people we say we are trying to reach will never come to a church to see a lot of amateur actors putting on a home talent show* [emphasis added].

I tell you, outside of politics there is not another field of activity that has more words and fewer deeds, more wind and less rain. What are we going to do about this awesome, beautiful worship that God calls for?[84]

Tozer's sincere questions have gone unanswered for decades and his observations unheeded. Yet in a few spots the light may have broken through.

David Platt, pastor of The Church at Brook Hills in Birmingham, Alabama, from 2006 to 2014, attempted a bold experiment. In an attempt to test the premise that the Word of

---

[84] A. W. Tozer, *Whatever Happened to Worship? A Call to True Worship* (Moody Publishers), Kindle Edition (2012).

God is enough, they stripped away from public worship any entertainment value and invited people to come simply to study God's Word.

> They called it Secret Church. They set a date—on a Friday night—when they would gather from 6:00 in the evening until midnight, and for six hours they would do nothing but study God's Word and pray. People came. A thousand people came the first time and it grew from that. Soon, they had to start taking reservations because the church was packed full. Secret Church now draws tens of thousands of people via simulcast in over 50 countries around the world—with no entertainment, no bells and whistles or smoke machines.[85]

When asked, "Why do they come?" Platt explained: "People are hungry for the Word. There's really nothing special or creative about it. It's just the study of the Word. . . . *The Word itself does the work!*" absent what Tozer in 1962 called "religious toys and trifles."[86]

It is important to note that this concluding discussion about "where is it all going—where will it end?" is not only about worship styles or music—the issue is not traditional versus contemporary versus blended worship, or organ versus worship band, though those elements certainly play into the discussion. As Livingstone adds, "That discussion misses the point completely." The preeminent issue is biblical worship—its meaning, its sacredness, its intent, its acceptable form, its setting, and most importantly, the object of our worship.

---

[85] *Ibid*, Livingstone.

[86] *Ibid.*

Tozer said it a half century ago that, even then, it was "scarcely possible in most places to get anyone to attend a meeting where the only attraction was God." More recently, David Platt has asked:

> What if we take away the cool music and the cushioned chairs?
> What if the screens are gone and the stage is no longer decorated?
> What if the air conditioning is off and the comforts are removed?
> Would His Word still be enough for his people to come together? Would it be enough?[87]

To which Tozer had already replied prophetically, "Heresy of method may be as deadly as heresy of message."[88]

"Yet," some would say, "our methods are attracting and winning people!" Again, Tozer seemingly anticipated the question with this answer: "Winning them to what? To true discipleship? To cross-carrying? To self-denial? To separation from the world? To crucifixion of the flesh? To holy living? To nobility of character? To a despising of the world's treasures? To hard self-discipline? To love for God? To total committal to Christ?"[89]

For Tozer, the survival of the church and the primary reason for its existence depended on getting one thing right:

> Yes, worship of the loving God is man's whole reason for existence. That is why we are born, and

---

[87] *Ibid*, Livingstone.

[88] *Ibid*, Tozer.

[89] *Ibid*.

that is why we are born again from above. That is why we were created, and that is why we have been recreated. That is why there was a genesis at the beginning, and that is why there is a re-genesis, called regeneration. That is also why there is a church. The Christian church exists to worship God first of all. Everything else must come second or third or fourth or fifth. . . .

Sad, sad indeed, are the cries of so many today who have never discovered why they were born. . . .

I was created to worship and praise God. I was redeemed that I should worship Him and enjoy Him forever. That is the primary issue, my brother or sister. . . .

You were created to worship. God wants you to know His redemption so you will desire to worship and praise Him.[90]

And can it be . . .

"We need to recognize that much of the attraction of contemporary worship comes from the fact it has taken the best the world has to offer but in so doing it has abandoned the orthodox, or right worship, God wants from us."[91] Where is your church with regard to "right worship"—that is, worship "according to the pattern"?

---

[90] *Ibid*, Tozer.

[91] *Ibid*, Arakaki.

12

Test Your Church

There are many styles and formats for worship, found in an equal number of churches in many denominations. All may have their place. All may have proper intentions and proceed toward a proper end. I am not the judge of what is proper and worshipful. There may even be other scriptural patterns for worship other than the passage in Isaiah 6. However, that particular illustration (Isaiah's experience) seems to me to be a good place to begin in evaluating the worship experience of your church.

Does the worship service begin by "calling you to worship"? There are as many ways to do this as there are Sundays. It can be done with a splendid choral introit sung by a choir or a simple spoken word. "Come, now is the time to worship" or "Come into His presence with thanksgiving." The recognition that God is present, waiting to receive our worship, is a profound way to begin every time, regardless of how it is communicated. It sets apart the time of worship from every other time and activity.

As you are called to worship, are you invited to witness the splendor of God as you come into His presence? As you are called into worship, is your attention drawn to the awesomeness of God? Are you encouraged to experience the breathtaking splendor of His presence? Are you invited to witness the majesty of His works? Anything else seems to miss the purpose of worship. "Holy, holy, holy is the Lord God Almighty, the whole earth is filled with His glory."

Does the music in your worship service invite your participation or is it more a performance? Do you find yourself standing, listening, but not singing? Do you want to harmonize with the melody, but find it difficult? Does the percussion overwhelm the music or support it? Is the music uncomfortably loud? (Having the ushers hand out earplugs as you enter might provide a clue.)

Does your worship include a time for confession of sins, corporate and/or personal? This one may be a stretch for some but no less essential each time we gather for worship. The form is not important here. Confession may be via written prayers, extemporaneous prayers, or silent and unspoken prayers. It is not the form that is important. Our church includes a written corporate prayer of confession each week read by one of the pastors. This bothers some (written prayers are a challenge for those from a low-church background). And furthermore, who is to be the arbiter of what I need to confess? Each week, the corporate prayer of confession is followed by a time of silence during which time each individual is invited to bring his or her personal sins before the Lord in seeking forgiveness. I must confess that as a member of the choir, I occasionally find myself sneaking a peak at the audience during this time. Curiously, I see many just looking around, obviously not in need of personal repentance—or maybe they came to church all prayed up.

Is confession followed by an acknowledgement of forgiveness of sins (an assurance of pardon) because of the work of Christ? This one is just as important as the time for confession. It never gets repetitious for me to have the pastor declare after the time of silent confession: "Hear the good news. In Jesus Christ you and I are forgiven" (or something similar that includes those words), to which a few of us more liturgical folks respond: "Thanks be to God!"

Is the spoken word (preaching) based on Scripture? For a layman, I know that this question approaches meddling, or worse. After all, what basis do I have for questioning a minister of the Gospel? A young person of our acquaintance offered this unsolicited observation after attending, on different Sundays, both our worship service and that of another large church: "Your pastor explains the Scripture clearly," she said, while adding, "he doesn't skip all around using many Scriptures trying to make his point."

Is there a place in your worship for a personal response to the spoken word? Is there a challenge to commitment? Is there opportunity to accept the call to go? It may be an uncomfortable time for some—that time at the end of the service when one is asked to respond, but it's no less important.

Is what we do in general in worship supported in Scripture? In addition to the evaluation of your worship experience as compared to the form or pattern of Isaiah chapter 6 (aspects of worship that I believe are essential), the following questions address other issues that may be an indication of creeping secularism within your church. The fact that they are present may or may not be indicative of anything other than that—creeping secularism.

Do folks "dress up" for church? Perhaps another way of asking this is "do folks wear something different on Sunday than on any week day or on Friday night?" Why is this important, or is it important? Admittedly, I can find no biblical injunction to dress up for church anywhere in Scripture (David was said to have danced "unclothed" before the Lord, embarrassing his wife and bringing shame on himself.[92]) Dressing up is simply a matter of respect shown for the institution (the church) and for our peers. The way one presents himself or herself communicates volumes about how one views his or her circumstances, and what one thinks about others who join with us in worship.

More importantly, how one dresses or grooms himself or herself says everything about how we think about the person into whose company we are about to appear. No one would show up for an audience with the Queen of England dressed in shorts or a T-shirt or in mismatched pants and a coat, no one that is who was still possessed of his or her senses and desired to show honor to royalty. How can anything less be acceptable in the church?

Worship brings us into the presence of the King of glory. The injunction "dress like it" seems to be unnecessary, does it not? Yet it seems today that there needs to be a sign at the entrance that goes something like this: "You are entering into the presence of the Almighty God, the High King of heaven. Does your

---

[92] 2 Samuel 6:14, 16: "*And David danced before the LORD with all his might; and David was girded with a linen ephod. . . . Michal Saul's daughter looked through a window, and saw king David leaping and dancing before the LORD; and she despised him in her heart*" (KJV).

appearance reflect that fact?" Instead, it seems that most see only the sign that says: "Come just as you are," believing that it refers to outward appearances only.

Do the ushers offer earplugs to those entering for worship? I have to admit that this question is a bit facetious and cynical on the surface. The important fact is not whether or not earplugs are offered, but that they should even be a consideration in the first place. We enter (or should enter) worship with anticipation, reverence, and awe, not with the concern or need to protect ourselves from potential auditory insult and injury.

When the audience is invited to sing, do a majority of folks sing heartfully or do they simply stand and listen? It only takes a few seconds to determine if your church welcomes participation during the singing. Just look around. Are folks singing or are they standing and listening?

Does the audience include folks of all age groups? By itself, this question seems out of place in a serious discussion of worship. Children's church and Sunday school opening exercises certainly teach children the values of worship and provide for them the experience of worship. The point is not that separate services for kids are wrong, but rather to underscore the fact that segregation by age groups in not necessarily a good thing. What is it about the music, liturgy, and preaching of the Word that is not right for children? Nothing, in my opinion. The experience of being included communicates something valuable to kids.

We would like to hear from you.

Contact Dr. Fessenden via email at ron@tgbtgbooks.com.

Appendix A

I'm not asking you to take them out of the world, but to keep them safe from the evil one. They do not belong to this world any more than I do. Make them holy by your truth; teach them your word, which is truth. Just as you sent me into the world, I am sending them into the world (John 17:15–18, NLT).

*M*any Christians today hold to a "two kingdom" philosophy. They live in the kingdom of this world while hoping for the Kingdom of God to come, not realizing that when Jesus ushered in the Kingdom of God over 2000 years ago, it did not go away. They worship as Christians utilizing all of the trappings of the kingdom of this world. While professing faith in Jesus, as aspiring citizens hoping for the return of the Kingdom of God, their worship (as well as their lifestyles) is ordered by secular values—that is, attitudes, activities, and influences that have no spiritual basis.

What follows are several Scripture passages that affirm that the Kingdom of God is here and help you discern your own place in it.

*The time is fulfilled, and the **kingdom of God** is at hand: repent ye, and believe the gospel* (Mark 1:15, KJV, emphasis added).

*And it came to pass afterward, that he went throughout every city and village, preaching and shewing the glad tidings of the **kingdom of God*** (Luke 8:1, emphasis added).

*Until John the Baptist, the law of Moses and the messages of the prophets were your guides. But now the Good News of the **Kingdom of God** is preached, and everyone is eager to get in* (Luke 16:16, NLT, emphasis added).

*Once, on being asked by the Pharisees when the **kingdom of God** would come, Jesus replied, "The coming of the **kingdom of God** is not something that can be observed, nor will people say, 'Here it is,' or 'There it is,' because the **kingdom of God** is in your midst"* (Luke 17:20–21, NIV, emphasis added).

Do not deceive yourselves. If any of you think you are wise by the standards of this age, he should become "fools" so that you may become wise (1 Corinthians 3:18, NIV).

Let nothing be done through selfish ambition or conceit, but in lowliness of mind let each esteem others better than himself. Let each of you look out not only for his own interests, but also for the interests of others (Philippians 2:3–4, NKJV).

For whoever wants to save their life will lose it, but whoever loses their life for me will save it. What good is it for someone to gain the whole world, and yet lose or forfeit their very self? Whoever is ashamed of me and my words, the Son of Man will be ashamed of them when he comes in his glory and in the glory of the Father and of the holy angels (Luke 9:24–26, NIV).

Do not lay up for yourselves treasures on earth, where moth and rust destroy and where thieves break in and steal; but lay up for yourselves treasures in heaven, where neither moth nor rust destroys and where thieves do not break in and steal. For where your treasure is, there your heart will be also (Matthew 6:19–21, NKJV).

Enter through the narrow gate. For wide is the gate and broad is the road that leads to destruction, and many enter through it. But small is the gate and narrow the road that leads to life, and only a few find it (Matthew 7:13–14, NIV).

We are citizens of the Kingdom of God. May our corporate worship always reflect our values and privileges as citizens of that Kingdom, eschewing anything and everything that is of the kingdom of this world.

About the Author

Ron Fessenden, MD, MPH, is a retired medical doctor. He received his MD from the University of Kansas School of Medicine in 1970 and his Masters in Public Health from the University of Hawaii School of Public Health in 1982.

For the past several years, Dr. Fessenden has been researching, writing, and speaking about the health benefits of consuming honey. He has given presentations at more than fifty venues across the United States and Canada about this topic, including a presentation entitled "Living Healthier – Aging Well with Honey" delivered at the Excellence in Aging Care Symposium in Fredericton, New Brunswick, in 2012 and in 2014.

In addition to his focus on proper nutrition for the brain, Dr. Fessenden is an avid runner, having completed eight marathons. On September 7, 2015, he completed his most recent marathon at the age of seventy.

His previously published works include:

The Honey Revolution – Restoring the Health of Future Generations, by Ron Fessenden, MD, MPH and Mike McInnes, MRPS, (WorldClassEmprise, LLC, 2008)

The Honey Revolution – Abridged, by Ron Fessenden, MD, MPH and Mike McInnes, MRPS, (WorldClassEmprise, LLC, 2010)

Feed Your Brain First, The Honey Revolution Series – Part 3, by Ronald E Fessenden, MD, MPH, (TGBTGBooks.com, LLC, 2013)

The New Honey Revolution, by Ronald E Fessenden, MD, MPH, (TGBTGBooks.com, LLC, 2014)

Of Gnats and Camels—and Other Things I Never Learned in Medical School, by Ronald E Fessenden, MD, MPH, (TGBTGBooks.com, LLC, 2016)

For more information go to:
www.tgbtgbooks.com

or email Dr. Fessenden at
ron@tgbtgbooks.com

CPSIA information can be obtained
at www.ICGtesting.com
Printed in the USA
BVOW11s2023301117
501453BV00001B/164/P